WRIGHT FAMILY RECORDS

DEEDS, 1790–1876; LAND TAX LISTS, 1791–1860; DEATHS, 1854–1896; PROBATES, 1790–1870

PATRICK COUNTY, VIRGINIA

∂∽∂

Robert N. Grant

Heritage Books
2025

HERITAGE BOOKS
AN IMPRINT OF HERITAGE BOOKS, INC.

Books, CDs, and more—Worldwide

For our listing of thousands of titles see our website
at
www.HeritageBooks.com

Published 2025 by
HERITAGE BOOKS, INC.
Publishing Division
5810 Ruatan Street
Berwyn Heights, MD 20740

International Standard Book Number
Paperbound: 978-0-7884-5060-0

Heritage Books by Robert N. Grant

Lynchburg

Wright Family Records: Lynchburg, Virginia Birth Records (1853–1896), Marriage Records (1805–1900), Marriage Notices (1794–1880), Census Records (1900), Deed Records (1805–1900), Death Records (1853–1896), Probate Records (1805–1900)

Amherst County

Wright Family Birth Records, 1853–1896; Marriage Records, 1761–1900; Census Records, 1810–1900, in Amherst County, Virginia

Wright Family Land Tax Records: Amherst County, Virginia, 1782–1850

Wright Family Patent Deeds and Land Grants, 1761–1900, Deed Records, 1761–1903; Chancery Court Files, 1804–1900; Death Records, 1853–1920; Cemetery Records by Cemetery; and Probate Records, 1761–1900, in Amherst County, Virginia

Wright Family Personal Property Tax Lists: Amherst County, Virginia, 1782–1850

Appomattox County

Wright Family Birth Records, Marriage Records, and Personal Property Tax Lists: Appomattox County, Virginia

Wright Family Census Records, Deed Records, Land Tax Lists, Death Records and Probate Records: Appomattox County, Virginia

Bedford County

Wright Family Census Records: Bedford County, Virginia, 1810–1900

Wright Family Death, Cemetery and Probate Records: Bedford County, Virginia

Wright Family Land Records: Bedford County, Virginia

Wright Family Personal Property Tax Records for Bedford County, Virginia, 1782 to 1850

Wright Family Records: Births in Bedford County, Virginia

Wright Family Records: Land Tax List, Bedford County, Virginia, 1782–1850

Wright Family Records: Marriages in Bedford County, Virginia

Botetourt County

Wright Family Birth, Marriage, and Personal Property Tax Records: Botetourt County, Virginia

Wright Family Census, Deed, Land Tax, Death and Probate Records: Botetourt County, Virginia

Campbell County

Wright Family Birth Records (1853–1896) and Marriage Records (1782–1900): Campbell County, Virginia

Wright Family Census Records: Campbell County, Virginia, 1810–1900

Wright Family Death Records (1853–1920), Cemetery Records by Cemetery, and Probate Records (1782–1900): Campbell County, Virginia

Wright Family Deed Records (1782–1900) and Land Tax List (1782–1850): Campbell County, Virginia

Wright Family Personal Property Tax Lists: Campbell County, Virginia, 1785–1850

Cumberland County

Wright Family Birth, Marriage, Personal Property Tax and Census Records, Cumberland County, Virginia

Wright Family Deed, Land Tax, Death and Probate Records, Cumberland County, Virginia

WRIGHT FAMILY RECORDS

DEED RECORDS

1790 TO 1876

PATRICK COUNTY, VIRGINIA

Revised as of January 12, 2025

<u>Introduction To Appendix: Deed Records for Patrick County, Virginia</u>

This document is an appendix to a larger work titled <u>Sorting Some Of The Wrights Of Southern Virginia</u>. The work is divided into parts for each family of Wrights that has been researched. Each part is divided into two sections; the first section is text discussing the family and the evidence supporting the relationships and the second section is a descendants chart summarizing the relationships and information known about each individual.

The appendices to the work (of which this document is one) present source records for persons named Wright by county and by type of record with the identification of the person named and their Wright ancestors to the extent known.

The source for the records listed in this appendix is the following:

1) Patrick County, Virginia, Deed Records, available from the Clerk of the Circuit Court, P.O. Box 148, 24171-0148, Stuart, Virginia 24171-0148.

The identification of a person or their ancestor by year and county indicates their year of death and county of residence at death. For example, "1763 Thomas Wright of Bedford County" indicates that this was the Thomas Wright who died in 1763 in Bedford County. If no state is listed after the county, the state is Virginia; counties in states other than Virginia will have a state listed after the county, as in "1876 William S. Wright of Highland County, Ohio".

A parenthetical after the name indicates an identification of the person when a place of death is not yet known, as in "John Wright (Goochland County Carpenter)". A county in parentheses after the name indicates the county with which that person was most identified when no evidence of the place of death has yet been found, as in "Grief Wright (Bedford County)".

All or portions of the text and descendants charts for each Wright family identified are available from the author:

Robert N. Grant
15 Campo Bello Court   (H) 650-854-0895
Menlo Park, California 94025   RNGrant@grantandgordon.com

This is a work in progress and I would be most interested in receiving additional information about any of the persons identified in these records in order to correct any errors or expand on the information given.

Appendix: Patrick County, Virginia, Deed Records

Book/Page		Date	Grantor	Grantee	Instrument	Identification
001	163	1794/03/29	John Wright	George Hairston	Deed	
003	165	1808/04/29	Reubin Short et al	Robert Wright	Deed	1809 Robert Wright of Patrick County, son of _____ Wright and Mary (_____) Wright
005	274	1819/03/20	Elisha Packwood et al	Jacob Wright	Deed	
006	103	1821/11/15	Jacob Wright	John A. Hairston Tr.	D of T	Jacob Wright, son of 1795 Joshua Wright of Rockingham County, North Carolina, and grandson of 1747 Edward Wright of Dorchester County, Maryland
006	284	1822/12/22	Jacob Wright	Richard M. Talefaro Tr.	D of T	Jacob Wright, son of 1795 Joshua Wright of Rockingham County, North Carolina, and grandson of 1747 Edward Wright of Dorchester County, Maryland
005	428	1823/03/04	Samuel C. Morriss	Robert Wright	Deed	1847 Robert Wright of Patrick County, son of 1811 William Wright of Pittsylvania County and grandson of 1755 John Wright of Lunenburg County
006	350	1824/10/20	John N. Wright & Nancy Wright & John Clark & Elizabeth Clark & Josiah Wright & Susannah Wright & Henry Crum & Mary Crum & Fanny Wright	William Canady	Deed	Children of 1809 Robert Wright of Patrick County and grandchildren of _____ Wright and Mary (_____) Wright
006	488	1825/08/10	Dandridge Slaughter	Robert Wright	Deed	1847 Robert Wright of Patrick County, son of 1811 William Wright of Pittsylvania County and grandson of 1755 John Wright of Lunenburg County

Appendix: Patrick County, Virginia, Deed Records

Book/Page	Date	Grantor	Grantee	Instrument	Identification
006 509	1825/12/01	Robert Wright	Notley Adams	Deed	1847 Robert Wright of Patrick County, son of 1811 William Wright of Pittsylvania County and grandson of 1755 John Wright of Lunenburg County
006 466	1826/02/08	Jacob Wright & Hannah Wright	William Via	Deed	Jacob Wright, son of 1795 Joshua Wright of Rockingham County, North Carolina, and grandson of 1747 Edward Wright of Dorchester County, Maryland
007 080	1828/08/13	John Wright	Jesse Corn Tr.	D of T	John N. Wright, son of 1809 Robert Wright of Patrick County and grandson of _____ Wright and Mary (_____) Wright
007 305	1830/01/16	Samuel H. Ferguson & Mary Ferguson	Sarah Wright	Deed	Sarah (_____) Wright, wife of 1809 Robert Wright of Patrick County, a son of _____ Wright and Mary (_____) Wright
007 306	1830/01/16	Samuel H. Ferguson & Mary Ferguson	Reuben Wright	Deed	1872 Reuben Wright of Patrick County, son of 1809 Robert Wright of Patrick County and grandson of _____ Wright and Mary (_____) Wright
007 307	1830/01/16	Reuben Wright	William Canaday	Deed	1872 Reuben Wright of Patrick County, son of 1809 Robert Wright of Patrick County and grandson of _____ Wright and Mary (_____) Wright
008 258	1833/09/19	Lewis D. Hancock	Robert Wright	Deed	1847 Robert Wright of Patrick County, son of 1811 William Wright of Pittsylvania County and grandson of 1755 John Wright of Lunenburg County
008 370	1834/05/19	Robert Wright	Hirum D. Wright	Deed	Grantor: 1847 Robert Wright of Patrick County son of 1811 William Wright of Pittsylvania County and grandson of 1755 John Wright of Lunenburg County Grantee: 1887 Hiram D. Wright of Patrick County, son of 1847 Robert Wright of Patrick County, grandson of 1811 William Wright of Pittsylvania County, and great grandson of 1755 John Wright of Lunenburg County

Appendix: Patrick County, Virginia, Deed Records

Book/Page	Date	Grantor	Grantee	Instrument	Identification
008 371	1834/04/12	Charles Hancock	James Wright	Deed	James T. Wright, son of 1847 Robert Wright of Patrick County, grandson of 1811 William Wright of Pittsylvania County, and great grandson of 1755 John Wright of Lunenburg County
009 392	1836/09/07	James T. Wright	Hiram D. Wright	Deed	Grantor: James T. Wright, son of 1847 Robert Wright of Patrick County, grandson of 1811 William Wright of Pittsylvania County, and great grandson of 1755 John Wright of Lunenburg County Grantee: 1887 Hiram D. Wright of Patrick County, son of 1847 Robert Wright of Patrick County, grandson of 1811 William Wright of Pittsylvania County, and great grandson of 1755 John Wright of Lunenburg County
009 408	1836/10/04	Hiram D. Wright & Mary Wright	Christopher Nicholes	Deed	1887 Hiram D. Wright of Patrick County, son of 1847 Robert Wright of Patrick County, grandson of 1811 William Wright of Pittsylvania County, and great grandson of 1755 John Wright of Lunenburg County
009 491	1837/03/04	Archibald Auxly & Lucy Auxly	James T. Wright	Deed	James T. Wright, son of 1847 Robert Wright of Patrick County, grandson of 1811 William Wright of Pittsylvania County, and great grandson of 1755 John Wright of Lunenburg County
009 477	1837/03/10	T. H. & B. Watkins	James T. Wright	Deed	James T. Wright, son of 1847 Robert Wright of Patrick County, grandson of 1811 William Wright of Pittsylvania County, and great grandson of 1755 John Wright of Lunenburg County
010 401	1838/02/28	Gabriel Dehart	Salley Wright	Deed	Sarah (____) Wright, wife of 1809 Robert Wright of Patrick County, a son of ____ Wright and Mary (____) Wright

Appendix: Patrick County, Virginia, Deed Records

Book/Page	Date	Grantor	Grantee	Instrument	Identification
010 389	1840/02/09	Robert Wright	Hiram D. Wright	Deed	Grantor: 1847 Robert Wright of Patrick County, son of 1811 William Wright of Pittsylvania County and grandson of 1755 John Wright of Lunenburg County Grantee: 1887 Hiram D. Wright of Patrick County, son of 1847 Robert Wright of Patrick County, grandson of 1811 William Wright of Pittsylvania County, and great grandson of 1755 John Wright of Lunenburg County
011 101	1841/11/13	Josiah Wright	John Turner Tr.	D of T	Josiah Wright son of 1809 Robert Wright of Patrick County and grandson of _____ Wright and Mary (_____) Wright
011 087	1841/09/02	Sarah Wright	Reuben Wright	Deed	Grantor: Sarah (_____) Wright, wife of 1809 Robert Wright of Patrick County, a son of _____ Wright and Mary (_____) Wright Grantee: 1872 Reuben Wright of Patrick County, son of 1809 Robert Wright of Patrick County and grandson of _____ Wright and Mary (_____) Wright
011 173	1842/03/23	Sarah Wright	William D. Young	Deed	Sarah (_____) Wright, wife of 1809 Robert Wright of Patrick County, a son of _____ Wright and Mary (_____) Wright
011 174	1842/03/23	Sarah Wright	Henry Crum	Deed	Sarah (_____) Wright, wife of 1809 Robert Wright of Patrick County, a son of _____ Wright and Mary (_____) Wright
011 223	1842/09/10	Sarah Wright	William D. Young	Deed	Sarah (_____) Wright, wife of 1809 Robert Wright of Patrick County, a son of _____ Wright and Mary (_____) Wright
011 458	1843/03/07	James T. Wright & Francis A. Wright	Marshall Wade	Deed	James T. Wright, son of 1847 Robert Wright of Patrick County, grandson of 1811 William Wright of Pittsylvania County, and great grandson of 1755 John Wright of Lunenburg County

Appendix: Patrick County, Virginia, Deed Records

Book/Page	Date	Grantor	Grantee	Instrument	Identification
011 559	1843/11/26	Hiram D. Wright	Robert Wright	Deed	1887 Hiram D. Wright of Patrick County, son of 1847 Robert Wright of Patrick County, grandson of 1811 William Wright of Pittsylvania County, and great grandson of 1755 John Wright of Lunenburg County
013 118	1848/04/24	Abram Spencer	Josiah Wright	Deed	1862 Josiah Wright of Patrick County, son of John N. Wright, grandson of 1809 Robert Wright of Patrick County, and great grandson of ____ Wright and Mary (____) Wright
013 130	1848/04/27	Henry Crum	Reubin Wright	Deed	1872 Reuben Wright of Patrick County, son of 1809 Robert Wright of Patrick County and grandson of ____ Wright and Mary (____) Wright
013 583	1850/11/01	Jubal Wright & Emily Wright	John Lackey Tr.	D of T	1868 Jubal Wright of Patrick County, son of John N. Wright, grandson of 1809 Robert Wright of Patrick County, and great grandson of ____ Wright and Mary (____) Wright
015 370	1851/03/18	Robert Hirston et al	Amanda V. Wright	Deed	Hannah Amanda V. (Kasey) Wright, wife of 1877 Bartlett Wright of Bedford County, a son of Grief Wright (Bedford County)
014 308	1852/09/01	John N. Wright & Nancy Wright	Martin Wright & Mary Wright & Jubul Wright & Josiah Wright & Turner Wright	Deed	Grantor: John N. Wright, son of 1809 Robert Wright of Patrick County and grandson of ____ Wright and Mary (____) Wright Grantees: Children of John N. Wright, grandchildren of 1809 Robert Wright of Patrick County, and great grandchildren of ____ Wright and Mary (____) Wright

Appendix: Patrick County, Virginia, Deed Records

Book/Page	Date	Grantor	Grantee	Instrument	Identification
014 389	1853/05/19	John N. Wright & Nancy Wright	Martin Wright & Mary Wright & Jabel Wright & Josiah Wright & Turner Wright	Deed	Grantor: John N. Wright, son of 1809 Robert Wright of Patrick County and grandson of ____ Wright and Mary (____) Wright Grantees: Children of John N. Wright, grandchildren of 1809 Robert Wright of Patrick County, and great grandchildren of ____ Wright and Mary (____) Wright
015 041	1854/05/31	Henry Crum & Polly Crum	Reuben Wright	Deed	1872 Reuben Wright of Patrick County, son of 1809 Robert Wright of Patrick County and grandson of ____ Wright and Mary (____) Wright
016 131	1857/01/17	Bartlet Wright & Hannah A. Wright et al	Mary Freeman	Deed	1877 Bartlett Wright of Bedford County, son of Grief Wright (Bedford County)
019 479	1857/01/17	Bartlett Wright & Hannah A. V. Wright & John N. Kasey & Elizabeth Kasey & Mary Freeman & Newton Kasey & Deborah Kasey & Clementine Kasey & Green B. Martin & Naoma Martin	W. C. Kasey	Deed	1877 Bartlett Wright of Bedford County, son of Grief Wright (Bedford County)
016 138	1857/11/10	James P. Martin & Martha Martin	Jubal Wright	Deed	1868 Jubal Wright of Patrick County, son of John N. Wright, grandson of 1809 Robert Wright of Patrick County, and great grandson of ____ Wright and Mary (____) Wright

Appendix: Patrick County, Virginia, Deed Records

Book/Page	Date	Grantor	Grantee	Instrument	Identification
016 258	1858/02/11	William Shelton et al	Hiram D. Wright	Deed	1887 Hiram D. Wright of Patrick County, son of 1847 Robert Wright of Patrick County, grandson of 1811 William Wright of Pittsylvania County, and great grandson of 1755 John Wright of Lunenburg County
016 539	1859/09/20	Jubal Wright	John Lackey Tr.	D of T	1868 Jubal Wright of Patrick County, son of John N. Wright and grandson of 1809 Robert Wright of Patrick County, and great grandson of ____ Wright and Mary (____) Wright
017 022	1860/02/10	Jubal Wright	Stephen B. Chainey & Alexander C. Chainey	Deed	1868 Jubal Wright of Patrick County, son of John N. Wright, grandson of 1809 Robert Wright of Patrick County, and great grandson of ____ Wright and Mary (____) Wright
017 038	1860/05/00	Jubal Wright	John N. Wright	Deed	Grantor: 1868 Jubal Wright of Patrick County, son of John W. Wright, grandson of 1809 Robert Wright of Patrick County, and great grandson of ____ Wright and Mary (____) Wright Grantee: John N. Wright, son of 1809 Robert Wright of Patrick County and grandson of ____ Wright and Mary (____) Wright
017 173	1861/02/15	John N. Wright	M. F. Robertson Tr.	D of T	John N. Wright, son of 1809 Robert Wright of Patrick County, and grandson of ____ Wright and Mary (____) Wright
017 307	1862/07/23	John Martin & Eliza Martin	Reuben Wright	Deed	1872 Reuben Wright of Patrick County, son of 1809 Robert Wright of Patrick County and grandson of ____ Wright and Mary (____) Wright
018 330	1865/07/25	John Tuggle Sr.	James P. Wright	Deed	1889 James Patterson Wright of Patrick County, son of 1872 Reuben Wright of Patrick County and grandson of 1809 Robert Wright of Patrick County, and great grandson of ____ Wright and Mary (____) Wright

Appendix: Patrick County, Virginia, Deed Records

Book/Page	Date	Grantor	Grantee	Instrument	Identification
017 547	1866/01/02	John N. Wright	Martin Wright	Deed	Grantor: John N. Wright, son of 1809 Robert Wright of Patrick County and grandson of _____ Wright and Mary (_____) Wright Grantee: 1900 Martin Wright of Patrick County, son of John N. Wright, grandson of 1809 Robert Wright of Patrick County, and great grandson of _____ Wright and Mary (_____) Wright
018 119	1867/12/16	Reuben Wright & Delila Wright	General J. Wright & Jefferson N. Wright	Deed	Grantor: 1872 Reuben Wright of Patrick County, son of 1809 Robert Wright of Patrick County and grandson of _____ Wright and Mary (_____) Wright Grantees: 1906 General Jackson Wright of Patrick County and 1920 Jefferson Nash Wright of Patrick County, sons of 1872 Reuben Wright of Patrick County. grandsons of 1809 Robert Wright of Patrick County, and great grandson of _____ Wright and Mary (_____) Wright
018 513	1870/11/10	Samuel Sneed & Mary Sneed	William F. Wright	Deed	1920/21 William Floyd Wright (Patrick County), son of 1872 Reuben Wright of Patrick County and grandson of 1809 Robert Wright of Patrick County, and great grandson of _____ Wright and Mary (_____) Wright
019 305	1873/12/20	William F. Wright	Jefferson N. Wright	Agmt.	Grantor: 1920/21 William Floyd Wright (Patrick County), son of 1872 Reuben Wright of Patrick County, grandson of 1809 Robert Wright of Patrick County, and great grandson of _____ Wright and Mary (_____) Wright Grantee: 1920 Jefferson Nash Wright of Patrick County, son of 1872 Reuben Wright of Patrick County, grandson of 1809 Robert Wright of of Mecklenburg County, and great grandson of _____ Wright and Mary (_____) Wright

Book/Page	Date	Grantor	Grantee	Instrument	Identification
019 276	1874/01/03	America Wright & James P. Wright & Susan S. Wright & William F. Wright & General J. Wright & Squire G. Wright & Mary Wright & Jefferson N. Wright & Nancy J. Wright	Marshall C. Wright	Deed	Grantors: Children of 1920 Jefferson Nash Wright of Patrick County, grandchildren of 1872 Reuben Wright of Patrick County, great grandchildren of 1809 Robert Wright of Patrick County, and great great grandchildren of ____ Wright and Mary (____) Wright Grantee: 1914 Marshall C. Wright of Patrick County, son of 1872 Reuben Wright of Patrick County, grandson of 1809 Robert Wright of Patrick County, and great grandson of ____ Wright and Mary (____) Wright
019 278	1874/01/03	America Wright & James P. Wright & Marshall C. Wright & Mary Wright	Squire G. W. Wright	Deed	Grantors: Children of 1920 Jefferson Nash Wright of Patrick County, grandchildren of 1872 Reuben Wright of Patrick County, great grandchildren of 1809 Robert Wright of Patrick County, and great great grandchildren of ____ Wright and Mary (____) Wright Grantee: 1904 Squire Green Wright of Patrick County, son of 1872 Reuben Wright of Patrick County, grandson of 1809 Robert Wright of Patrick County, and great grandson of ____ Wright and Mary (____) Wright
019 209	1876/06/23	C. S. Tuggle	James P. Wright	Release	1889 James Patterson Wright of Patrick County, son of 1872 Reuben Wright of Patrick County, grandson of 1809 Robert Wright of Patrick County, and great grandson of ____ Wright and Mary (____) Wright

WRIGHT FAMILY RECORDS

LAND TAX LISTS

1791 TO 1860

PATRICK COUNTY, VIRGINIA

Revised as of January 12, 2025

<u>Introduction To Appendices: Land Tax Records, Patrick County, Virginia</u>

This document is an appendix to a larger work titled <u>Sorting Some Of The Wrights Of Southern Virginia</u>. The work is divided into parts for each family of Wrights that has been researched. Each part is divided into two sections; the first section is text discussing the family and the evidence supporting the relationships and the second section is a descendants chart summarizing the relationships and information known about each individual.

The appendices to the work (of which this document is one) present source records for persons named Wright by county and by type of record with the identification of the person named and their Wright ancestors to the extent known.

The source for the records listed in this appendix is the following:

    1)   Patrick County, Virginia, Land Tax Lists, available from The Library of Virginia, 800 East Broad Street, Richmond, Virginia 23219

The identification of a person or their ancestor by year and county indicates their year of death and county of residence at death. For example, "1763 Thomas Wright of Bedford County" indicates that this was the Thomas Wright who died in 1763 in Bedford County. If no state is listed after the county, the state is Virginia; counties in states other than Virginia will have a state listed after the county, as in "1876 William S. Wright of Highland County, Ohio".

A parenthetical after the name indicates an identification of the person when a place of death is not yet known, as in "John Wright (Goochland County Carpenter)". A county in parentheses after the name indicates the county with which that person was most identified when no evidence of the place of death has yet been found, 3as in "Grief Wright (Bedford County)".

All or portions of the text and descendants charts for each Wright family identified are available from the author:

    Robert N. Grant
    15 Campo Bello Court   (H) 650-854-0895
    Menlo Park, California 94025   RNGrant@grantandgordon.com

This is a work in process and I would be most interested in receiving additional information about any of the persons identified in these records in order to correct any errors or expand on the information given.

1791-1808 LAND TAX LIST

PATRICK COUNTY, VIRGINIA

Appendix: Patrick County, Virginia, 1791-1808 Land Tax List:

No Wrights listed

1809 LAND TAX LIST

PATRICK COUNTY, VIRGINIA

Appendix: Patrick County, Virginia, 1809 Land Tax List:

Persons Names Owning Land	Quantity of Land	Rate p Acre in Dollars & Cents	Total Amount in Dollars & Cents	Amount of tax in Dollars & Cents	Identification
Robert Wright	216	.78	168.48	.77	1809 Robert Wright of Patrick County, son of _____ Wright and Mary (_____) Wright

1810 LAND TAX LIST

PATRICK COUNTY, VIRGINIA

Appendix: Patrick County, Virginia, 1810 Land Tax List:

Persons Names Owning Land	Quantity of Land	Rate p Acre in Dollars & Cents	Total Amount in Dollars & Cents	Amount of tax in Dollars & Cents	Identification
Robert Wright	216	.78	168.48	.77	1809 Robert Wright of Patrick County, son of ____ Wright and Mary (____) Wright

1811 LAND TAX LIST

PATRICK COUNTY, VIRGINIA

Appendix: Patrick County, Virginia, 1811 Land Tax List:

Persons Names Owning Land	Quantity of Land	Rate p Acre in Dollars & Cents	Total Amount in Dollars & Cents	Amount of tax in Dollars & Cents	Identification
Robert Wright	216	.78	168.48	.77	1809 Robert Wright of Patrick County, son of _____ Wright and Mary (_____) Wright

1812 LAND TAX LIST

PATRICK COUNTY, VIRGINIA

Appendix: Patrick County, Virginia, 1812 Land Tax List:

Persons Names Owning Land	Quantity of Land	Rate p Acre in Dollars & Cents	Total Amount in Dollars & Cents	Amount of tax in Dollars & Cents	Identification
Robert Wright	216	.78	168.48	.77	1809 Robert Wright of Patrick County, son of _____ Wright and Mary (____) Wright

1813 LAND TAX LIST

PATRICK COUNTY, VIRGINIA

Appendix: Patrick County, Virginia, 1813 Land Tax List:

Persons names owning land	Quantity of land	Rate p Acre in Dollars and Cents	Total amt in Dollars & Cents	Amount of Taxes in Dollars & Cents	Situation	Identification
Robert Wright	216	.78	168.48	1.07¾	on the waters of Smiths River	1809 Robert Wright of Patrick County, son _____ Wright and Mary (_____) Wright

1814 LAND TAX LIST

PATRICK COUNTY, VIRGINIA

Appendix: Patrick County, Virginia, 1814 Land Tax List:

Name of the Owner	Residence	Estate	No of Acres of Land	Description of the Land	Distance & bearing from the Court House	rate of land p acre in D & Cts.	Total value of the land	Amt of tax 85¢ p $100	Total amt of tax upon the land
Robert Wright decd	Patrick	fee simple	216	Water Smiths river	20 miles North	.78	168.48	1.44	

Appendix: Patrick County, Virginia, 1814 Land Tax List:

Name of the Owner [cont'd from prior page]	Explanation of Alterations during the last Year &c	Identification
Robert Wright decd		1809 Robert Wright of Patrick County, son of _____ Wright and Mary (_____) Wright

1815 LAND TAX LIST

PATRICK COUNTY, VIRGINIA

Appendix: Patrick County, Virginia, 1815 Land Tax List:

Name of the Owner	Residence	Estate	No of Acres of Land	Description of the Land	Distance & bearing from the Court House	rate of land p acre in D & Cts.	Total value of the land	Amt of tax 85¢ p $100	Total amt of tax upon the land
Robert Wright decd	Patrick	fee simple	216	Water Smiths river	20 miles North	.78	168.48	1.44	

Appendix: Patrick County, Virginia, 1815 Land Tax List:

Name of the Owner [cont'd from prior page]	Explanation of Alterations during the last Year &c	Identification
Robert Wright decd		1809 Robert Wright of Patrick County, son of _____ Wright and Mary (_____) Wright

1816 LAND TAX LIST

PATRICK COUNTY, VIRGINIA

Appendix: Patrick County, Virginia, 1816 Land Tax List:

Name of the Owner	Residence	Estate	No of Acres of Land	Description of the Land	Distance & bearing from the Court House	rate of land p acre in D & Cts.	Total value of the land	Amt of tax 85¢ p $100	Total amt of tax upon the land
Robert Wright decd	Patrick	fee simple	216	Water Smiths river	20 miles North	.78	168.48	1.26	

Appendix: Patrick County, Virginia, 1816 Land Tax List:

Name of the Owner [cont'd from prior page]	Explanation of Alterations during the last Year &c	Identification
Robert Wright decd		1809 Robert Wright of Patrick County, son of _____ Wright and Mary (_____) Wright

1817 LAND TAX LIST

PATRICK COUNTY, VIRGINIA

Appendix: Patrick County, Virginia, 1817 Land Tax List:

Name of the Owner	Residence	Estate	No of Acres of Land	Description of the Land	Distance & bearing from the Court House	rate of land p acre in D & Cts.	Total value of the land	Amt of tax 85¢ p $100	Total amt of tax upon the land
Robert Wright decd	Patrick	fee simple	216	Water Smiths river					

Appendix: Patrick County, Virginia, 1817 Land Tax List:

Name of the Owner [cont'd from prior page]	Explanation of Alterations during the last Year &c	Identification
Robert Wright decd		1809 Robert Wright of Patrick County, son of _____ Wright and Mary (_____) Wright

1818 LAND TAX LIST

PATRICK COUNTY, VIRGINIA

Appendix: Patrick County, Virginia, 1818 Land Tax List:

Name of the Owner	Residence	Estate	No of Acres of Land	Description of the Land	Distance & bearing from the Court House	rate of land p acre in D & Cts.	Total value of the land	Amt of tax 85¢ p $100	Total amt of tax upon the land
Robert Wright decd	Patrick	fee simple	216	Water Smiths river	20 miles North	.78	168.48	1.26	

Appendix: Patrick County, Virginia, 1818 Land Tax List:

Name of the Owner [cont'd from prior page]	Explanation of Alterations during the last Year &c	Identification
Robert Wright decd		1809 Robert Wright of Patrick County, son of _____ Wright and Mary (_____) Wright

1819 LAND TAX LIST

PATRICK COUNTY, VIRGINIA

Appendix: Patrick County, Virginia, 1819 Land Tax List:

Name of the Owner	Residence	Estate	No of Acres of Land	Description of the Land	Distance & bearing from the Court House	rate of land p acre in D & Cts.	Total value of the land	Amt of tax 85¢ p $100	Total amt of tax upon the land
Robert Wright decd	Patrick	fee simple	216	Water Smiths river	20 N	.78	168.48	1.26	

Appendix: Patrick County, Virginia, 1819 Land Tax List:

Name of the Owner [cont'd from prior page]	Explanation of Alterations during the last Year &c	Identification
Robert Wright decd		1809 Robert Wright of Patrick County, son of _____ Wright and Mary (_____) Wright

1820 LAND TAX LIST

PATRICK COUNTY, VIRGINIA

Appendix: Patrick County, Virginia, 1820 Land Tax List:

Name of the Owner	Residence	Estate	No of Acres of Land	Description of the Land	Distance & bearing from the Court House	rate of land p acre in D & Cts.	Total value of the land	Amt of tax 85¢ p $100	Total amt of tax upon the land
Robert Wright decd	Patrick	In fee	216	Waters Smith river	20 N	1.62	229.50	.29	
Jacob Wright	Patrick	In fee	300	Smith river	___ NE	.70	210.00	.26	

Appendix: Patrick County, Virginia, 1820 Land Tax List:

Name of the Owner [cont'd from prior page]	Explanation of Alterations during the last Year &c	Identification
Robert Wright decd		1809 Robert Wright of Patrick County, son of _____ Wright and Mary (_____) Wright
Jacob Wright	Transferred from Elisha Packwood	Jacob Wright, son of 1795 Joshua Wright of Rockingham County, North Carolina, and grandson of 1747 Edward Wright of Dorchester County, Maryland

1821 LAND TAX LIST

PATRICK COUNTY, VIRGINIA

Appendix: Patrick County, Virginia, 1821 Land Tax List:

Name of the Owner	Residence	Estate	No of Acres of Land	Description of the Land	Distance & bearing from the Court House	rate of land p acre in D & Cts.	Total value of the land	Amt of tax 85¢ p $100	Total amt of tax upon the land
Robert Wright ___	Patrick	In fee	216	waters Smiths River	20 N.	1.06¼	229.50	.21	
Jacob Wright	Patrick	In fee	300	Smiths river	21 NE	.70	210.00	.19	

Appendix: Patrick County, Virginia, 1821 Land Tax List:

Name of the Owner [cont'd from prior page]	Explanation of Alterations during the last Year &c	Identification
Robert Wright ___		1809 Robert Wright of Patrick County, son of ____ Wright and Mary (____) Wright
Jacob Wright	Transferred from Elisha Packwood	Jacob Wright, son of 1795 Joshua Wright of Rockingham County, North Carolina, and grandson of 1747 Edward Wright of Dorchester County, Maryland

1822 LAND TAX LIST

PATRICK COUNTY, VIRGINIA

Appendix: Patrick County, Virginia, 1822 Land Tax List:

Name of the Owner	Residence	Estate	No of Acres of Land	Description of the Land	Distance & bearing from the Court House	rate of land p acre in D & Cts.	Total value of the land	Amt of tax 85¢ p $100	Total amt of tax upon the land
Robert Wright decd	Patrick	In fee	216	waters Smiths River	20 N.	1.06¼	229.50	.21	
Jacob Wright	Patrick	In fee	300	Smiths river	20 NE	.70	210.00	.19	

Appendix: Patrick County, Virginia, 1822 Land Tax List:

Name of the Owner [cont'd from prior page]	Explanation of Alterations during the last Year &c	Identification
Robert Wright decd		1809 Robert Wright of Patrick County, son of _____ Wright and Mary (_____) Wright
Jacob Wright		Jacob Wright, son of 1795 Joshua Wright of Rockingham County, North Carolina, and grandson of 1747 Edward Wright of Dorchester County, Maryland

1823 LAND TAX LIST

PATRICK COUNTY, VIRGINIA

Appendix: Patrick County, Virginia, 1823 Land Tax List:

Name of the Owner	Residence	Estate	No of Acres of Land	Description of the Land	Distance & bearing from the Court House	rate of land p acre in D & Cts.	Total value of the land	Amt of tax 85¢ p $100	Total amt of tax upon the land
Robert Wright dec	Patrick	In fee	216	waters Smiths River	20 N.	1.64	229.50	.19	
Jacob Wright	Patrick	In fee	300	Smiths River	20 NE	.70	210.00	.17	

Appendix: Patrick County, Virginia, 1823 Land Tax List:

Name of the Owner [cont'd from prior page]	Explanation of Alterations during the last Year &c	Identification
Robert Wright dec		1809 Robert Wright of Patrick County, son of ____ Wright and Mary (____) Wright
Jacob Wright		Jacob Wright, son of 1795 Joshua Wright of Rockingham County, North Carolina, and grandson of 1747 Edward Wright of Dorchester County, Maryland

1824 LAND TAX LIST

PATRICK COUNTY, VIRGINIA

Appendix: Patrick County, Virginia, 1824 Land Tax List:

Name of the Owner	Residence	Estate	No of Acres of Land	Description of the Land	Distance & bearing from the Court House	rate of land p acre in D & Cts.	Total value of the land	Amt of tax 85¢ p $100	Total amt of tax upon the land
Robert Wright dec	Patrick	In fee	216	waters Smiths River	20 N.	1.06¼	229.50	.19	
Jacob Wright	Patrick	In fee	300	Smiths River	20 NE	.70	210.00	.17	

Appendix: Patrick County, Virginia, 1824 Land Tax List:

Name of the Owner [cont'd from prior page]	Explanation of Alterations during the last Year &c	Identification
Robert Wright dec		1809 Robert Wright of Patrick County, son of ____ Wright and Mary (____) Wright
Jacob Wright		Jacob Wright, son of 1795 Joshua Wright of Rockingham County, North Carolina, and grandson of 1747 Edward Wright of Dorchester County, Maryland

1825 LAND TAX LIST

PATRICK COUNTY, VIRGINIA

Appendix: Patrick County, Virginia, 1825 Land Tax List:

Name of the Owner	Residence	Estate	No of Acres of Land	Description of the Land	Distance & bearing from the Court House	rate of land p acre in D & Cts.	Total value of the land	Amt of tax 85¢ p $100	Total amt of tax upon the land
Robert Wright dec	Patrick	In fee	176	waters Smiths River	20 N.	1.06¼	187.00	.14	
Jacob Wright	Patrick	In fee	300	Smiths River	20 NE	.70	210.00	.17	

Appendix: Patrick County, Virginia, 1825 Land Tax List:

Name of the Owner [cont'd from prior page]	Explanation of Alterations during the last Year &c	Identification
Robert Wright dec		1809 Robert Wright of Patrick County, son of _____ Wright and Mary (_____) Wright
Jacob Wright		Jacob Wright, son of 1795 Joshua Wright of Rockingham County, North Carolina, and grandson of 1747 Edward Wright of Dorchester County, Maryland

1826 LAND TAX LIST

PATRICK COUNTY, VIRGINIA

Appendix: Patrick County, Virginia, 1826 Land Tax List:

Name of the Owner	Residence	Estate	No of Acres of Land	Description of the Land	Distance & bearing from the Court House	rate of land p acre in D & Cts.	Total value of the land	Amt of tax 85¢ p $100	Total amt of tax upon the land
Robert Wright dec	Patrick	In fee	43	Waters Smiths River	20 N.	1.06¼	45.68	.04	
Jacob Wright	Patrick	In fee	300	Smiths River	20 NE	.70	210.00	.17	

Appendix: Patrick County, Virginia, 1826 Land Tax List:

Name of the Owner [cont'd from prior page]	Explanation of Alterations during the last Year &c	Identification
Robert Wright dec		1809 Robert Wright of Patrick County, son of _____ Wright and Mary (_____) Wright
Jacob Wright		Jacob Wright, son of 1795 Joshua Wright of Rockingham County, North Carolina, and grandson of 1747 Edward Wright of Dorchester County, Maryland

1827 LAND TAX LIST

PATRICK COUNTY, VIRGINIA

Appendix: Patrick County, Virginia, 1827 Land Tax List:

Name of the Owner	Residence	Estate	No of Acres of Land	Description of the Land	Distance & bearing from the Court House	rate of land p acre in D & Cts.	Total value of the land	Amt of tax 85¢ p $100	Total amt of tax upon the land
Robert Wright	Patrick	In fee	50	Waters Smiths River	20 N.	1.00	50.00	.04	
Robert Wright dec	Patrick	In fee	43	Water Smiths River	20 N	1.06¼	45.68	.04	

Appendix: Patrick County, Virginia, 1827 Land Tax List:

Name of the Owner [cont'd from prior page]	Explanation of Alterations during the last Year &c	Identification
Robert Wright	Transferred from Danridge Slaughter	1847 Robert Wright of Patrick County, son of 1811 William Wright of Pittsylvania County and grandson of 1755 John Wright of Lunenburg County
Robert Wright dec		1809 Robert Wright of Patrick County, son of ____ Wright and Mary (____) Wright

1828 LAND TAX LIST

PATRICK COUNTY, VIRGINIA

Appendix: Patrick County, Virginia, 1828 Land Tax List:

Name of the Owner	Residence	Estate	No of Acres of Land	Description of the Land	Distance & bearing from the Court House	rate of land p acre in D & Cts.	Total value of the land	Amt of tax 85¢ p $100	Total amt of tax upon the land
Robert Wright	Patrick	In fee	50	Waters Smiths River	12 N.	1.00	50.00	.04	
Robert Wright dec	Patrick	In fee	43	Water Smiths River	20 N	1.06¼	45.68	.04	

Appendix: Patrick County, Virginia, 1828 Land Tax List:

Name of the Owner [cont'd from prior page]	Explanation of Alterations during the last Year &c	Identification
Robert Wright		1847 Robert Wright of Patrick County, son of 1811 William Wright of Pittsylvania County and grandson of 1755 John Wright of Lunenburg County
Robert Wright dec		1809 Robert Wright of Patrick County, son of ____ Wright and Mary (____) Wright

1829 LAND TAX LIST

PATRICK COUNTY, VIRGINIA

Appendix: Patrick County, Virginia, 1829 Land Tax List:

Name of the Owner	Residence	Estate	No of Acres of Land	Description of the Land	Distance & bearing from the Court House	rate of land p acre in D & Cts.	Total value of the land	Amt of tax 85¢ p $100	Total amt of tax upon the land
Robert Wright	Patrick	In fee	50	Waters Smiths River	12 N.	1.00	50.00	.04	
Robert Wright dec	Patrick	In fee	43	Water Smiths River	20 N	1.62⅓	45.68	.04	

Appendix: Patrick County, Virginia, 1829 Land Tax List:

Name of the Owner [cont'd from prior page]	Explanation of Alterations during the last Year &c	Identification
Robert Wright		1847 Robert Wright of Patrick County, son of 1811 William Wright of Pittsylvania County and grandson of 1755 John Wright of Lunenburg County
Robert Wright dec		1809 Robert Wright of Patrick County, son of _____ Wright and Mary (_____) Wright

1830 LAND TAX LIST

PATRICK COUNTY, VIRGINIA

Appendix: Patrick County, Virginia, 1830 Land Tax List:

Name of the Owner	Residence	Estate	No of Acres of Land	Description of the Land	Distance & bearing from the Court House	rate of land p acre in D & Cts.	Total value of the land	Amt of tax 85¢ p $100	Total amt of tax upon the land
Robert Wright	Patrick	in fee	50	waters of Smiths River	12 NP.	1.00	50.00	.04	
Robert Wright dec	Patrick	in fee	43	Water Smiths River	20 N	1.06¼	45.68	.04	

Appendix: Patrick County, Virginia, 1830 Land Tax List:

Name of the Owner [cont'd from prior page]	Explanation of Alterations during the last Year &c	Identification
Robert Wright		1847 Robert Wright of Patrick County, son of 1811 William Wright of Pittsylvania County and grandson of 1755 John Wright of Lunenburg County
Robert Wright dec		1809 Robert Wright of Patrick County, son of _____ Wright and Mary (_____) Wright

1831 LAND TAX LIST

PATRICK COUNTY, VIRGINIA

Appendix: Patrick County, Virginia, 1831 Land Tax List:

Name of the Owner	Residence	Estate	No of Acres of Land	Description of the Land	Distance & bearing from the Court House	rate of land p acre in D & Cts.	Total value of the land	Amt of tax 85¢ p $100	Total amt of tax upon the land
Robert Wright	Patrick	in fee	50	waters of Smiths River	7 N	1.00	50.00	.04	
Sarah Wright	Patrick	in fee	97	waters of Smiths River	20 NE	1.00	94.00	.08	
Reuben Wright	Patrick	in fee	100	on Smiths river	Same	1.00	100.00	.08	

Appendix: Patrick County, Virginia, 1831 Land Tax List:

Name of the Owner [cont'd from prior page]	Explanation of Alterations during the last Year &c	Identification
Robert Wright	A tract of 43 acres transferred from Robert Wright Dec to Wm. Connady	1847 Robert Wright of Patrick County, son of 1811 William Wright of Pittsylvania County and grandson of 1755 John Wright of Lunenburg County [mistakenly attributed to 1809 Robert Wright deceased]
Sarah Wright	Transferred from Saml H Ferguson(?)	Sarah (____) Wright, wife of 1809 Robert Wright of Patrick County, a son of ____ Wright and Mary (____) Wright
Reuben Wright	Transfered from same	1872 Reuben Wright of Patrick County, son of 1809 Robert Wright of Patrick County and grandson of ____ Wright and Mary (____) Wright

1832 LAND TAX LIST

PATRICK COUNTY, VIRGINIA

Appendix: Patrick County, Virginia, 1832 Land Tax List:

Name of the Owner	Residence	Estate	No of Acres of Land	Description of the Land	Distance & bearing from the Court House	rate of land p acre in D & Cts.	Total value of the land	Amt of tax 85¢ p $100	Total amt of tax upon the land
Robert Wright	Patrick	in fee	50	waters of Smiths R	7 N	1.00	50.00	.04	
Sarah Wright	Patrick	in fee	97	waters of Smiths River	20 NE	1.00	97.00	.08	
Reuben Wright	Patrick	in fee	100	same	same	1.00	100.00	.08	

Appendix: Patrick County, Virginia, 1832 Land Tax List:

Name of the Owner [cont'd from prior page]	Explanation of Alterations during the last Year &c	Identification
Robert Wright		1847 Robert Wright of Patrick County, son of 1811 William Wright of Pittsylvania County and grandson of 1755 John Wright of Lunenburg County
Sarah Wright		Sarah (____) Wright, wife of 1809 Robert Wright of Patrick County, a son of ____ Wright and Mary (____) Wright
Reuben Wright		1872 Reuben Wright of Patrick County, son of 1809 Robert Wright of Patrick County and grandson of ____ Wright and Mary (____) Wright

1833 LAND TAX LIST

PATRICK COUNTY, VIRGINIA

Appendix: Patrick County, Virginia, 1833 Land Tax List:

Name of the Owner	Residence	Estate	No of Acres of Land	Description of the Land	Distance & bearing from the Court House	rate of land p acre in D & Cts.	Total value of the land	Amt of tax 85¢ p $100	Total amt of tax upon the land
Robert Wright	Patrick	in fee	50	waters Smiths R	7 N	1.00	50.00	.04	
Sarah Wright	Patrick	in fee	97	waters Smiths R	20 NE	1.00	97.00	.07	
Reuben Wright	Patrick	in fee	100	on Smiths R	20 NE	1.00	100.00	.08	

Appendix: Patrick County, Virginia, 1833 Land Tax List:

Name of the Owner [cont'd from prior page]	Explanation of Alterations during the last Year &c	Identification
Robert Wright		1847 Robert Wright of Patrick County, son of 1811 William Wright of Pittsylvania County and grandson of 1755 John Wright of Lunenburg County
Sarah Wright		Sarah (_____) Wright, wife of 1809 Robert Wright of Patrick County, a son of _____ Wright and Mary (_____) Wright
Reuben Wright		1872 Reuben Wright of Patrick County, son of 1809 Robert Wright of Patrick County and grandson of _____ Wright and Mary (_____) Wright

1834 LAND TAX LIST

PATRICK COUNTY, VIRGINIA

Appendix: Patrick County, Virginia, 1834 Land Tax List:

Name of the Owner	Residence	Estate	No of Acres of Land	Description of the Land	Distance & bearing from the Court House	rate of land p acre in D & Cts.	Total value of the land	Amt of tax 85¢ p $100	Total amt of tax upon the land
Robert Wright	Patrick	Fee	50	waters of Smiths R	7 N	1.00	50.00	.04	
Robert Wright	Patrick	Fee	106	Sycamor	__ N	25.00	26.50	.02	
Sarah Wright	Patrick	Fee	97	waters of Smiths R	20 NE	1.00	97.00	.08	
" "	"	"	75	" " "	" "	1.00	75.00	.06	
Reuben Wright	Patrick	Fee	100	Smiths R	20 NE	1.00	100.00	.08	

Appendix: Patrick County, Virginia, 1834 Land Tax List:

Name of the Owner [cont'd from prior page]	Explanation of Alterations during the last Year &c	Identification
Robert Wright		1847 Robert Wright of Patrick County, son of 1811 William Wright of Pittsylvania County and grandson of 1755 John Wright of Lunenburg County
Robert Wright	Transfer from L.DH Hancock	1847 Robert Wright of Patrick County, son of 1811 William Wright of Pittsylvania County and grandson of 1755 John Wright of Lunenburg County
Sarah Wright		Sarah (____) Wright, wife of 1809 Robert Wright of Patrick County, a son of 1819 Reuben Wright of Mecklenburg County
" "	New grant	
Reuben Wright		1872 Reuben Wright of Patrick County, son of 1809 Robert Wright of Patrick County and grandson of ____ Wright and Mary (____) Wright

1835 LAND TAX LIST

PATRICK COUNTY, VIRGINIA

Appendix: Patrick County, Virginia, 1835 Land Tax List:

Name of the Owner	Residence	Estate	No of Acres of Land	Description of the Land	Distance & bearing from the Court House	rate of land p acre in D & Cts.	Total value of the land	Amt of tax 85¢ p $100	Total amt of tax upon the land
Robert Wright	Patrick	in fee	50	waters Smiths River	7 N	1.50	50.00	.04	
Sarah Wright	Patrick	in fee	97	waters of Smiths R	20 NE	1.00	97.00	.08	
Same	"	" "	75	" " "	" "	1.00	75.00	.06	
Reubin Wright	Patrick	in fee	100	Smith River	20 NE	1.00	100.00	.08	
Hiram D Wright	Patrick	in fee	116	Rock castle(?)		.25	26.50	.02	

Appendix: Patrick County, Virginia, 1835 Land Tax List:

Name of the Owner [cont'd from prior page]	Explanation of Alterations during the last Year &c	Identification
Robert Wright	a tract conveyed to H D Wright	1847 Robert Wright of Patrick County, son of 1811 William Wright of Pittsylvania County and grandson of 1755 John Wright of Lunenburg County
Sarah Wright		Sarah (____) Wright, wife of 1809 Robert Wright of Patrick County, a son of ____ Wright and Mary (____) Wright
" "	New grant	
Reubin Wright		1872 Reuben Wright of Patrick County, son of 1809 Robert Wright of Patrick County and grandson of ____ Wright and Mary (____) Wright
Hiram D Wright	transfrd from Robert Wright	1887 Hiram D. Wright of Patrick County, son of 1847 Robert Wright of Patrick County, grandson of 1811 William Wright of Pittsylvania County, and great grandson of 1755 John Wright of Lunenburg County

1836 LAND TAX LIST

PATRICK COUNTY, VIRGINIA

Appendix: Patrick County, Virginia, 1836 Land Tax List:

Name of the Owner	Residence	Estate	No of Acres of Land	Description of the Land	Distance & bearing from the Court House	rate of land p acre in D & Cts.	Total value of the land	Amt of tax 85¢ p $100	Total amt of tax upon the land
Sarah Wright	Patrick	in fee	97	waters of Smiths R	20 NE	1.00	97.00	.08	
Same	"	" "	75	" " "	" "	1.00	75.00	.06	
Reubin Wright	Patrick	in fee	100	Smith River	20 NE	1.00	100.00	.08	
James T Wright	Patrick	in fee	112	Sycamore	N	.25	28.00	.02	
Hyram D Wright	Patrick	in fee	106	Sycamore		.25	26.50	.02	
Robert Wright	Patrick	in fee	50	waters Smiths R	7 N	1.00	50.00	.04	

Appendix: Patrick County, Virginia, 1836 Land Tax List:

Name of the Owner [cont'd from prior page]	Explanation of Alterations during the last Year &c	Identification
Sarah Wright Same		Sarah (____) Wright, wife of 1809 Robert Wright of Patrick County, a son of ____ Wright and Mary (____) Wright
Reubin Wright		1872 Reuben Wright of Patrick County, son of 1809 Robert Wright of Patrick County and grandson of ____ Wright and Mary (____) Wright
James T Wright		1875 James Tidwell Wright of Randolph County, Alabama, son of 1847 Robert Wright of Patrick County, grandson of 1811 William Wright of Pittsylvania County, and great grandson of 1755 John Wright of Lunenburg County
Hyram D Wright		1887 Hiram D. Wright of Patrick County, son of 1847 Robert Wright of Patrick County, grandson of 1811 William Wright of Pittsylvania County, and great grandson of 1755 John Wright of Lunenburg County
Robert Wright		1847 Robert Wright of Patrick County, son of 1811 William Wright of Pittsylvania County and grandson of 1755 John Wright of Lunenburg County

1837 LAND TAX LIST

PATRICK COUNTY, VIRGINIA

Appendix: Patrick County, Virginia, 1837 Land Tax List:

Name of the Owner	Residence	Estate	No of Acres of Land	Description of the Land	Distance & bearing from the Court House	rate of land p acre in D & Cts.	Total value of the land	Amt of tax 85¢ p $100	Total amt of tax upon the land
Sarah Wright	Patrick	in fee	97	Waters Smiths River	20 N	1.00	97.00	.08	
"	"	" "	75	" " "	" "	1.00	75.00	.06	
Reubin Wright	Patrick	in fee	100	Smith River	20 NE	1.00	100.00	.08	
James T Wright	Patrick	in fee	112	Sycamore	8 N	.25	28.00	.02	
Hyram D Wright	Patrick	in fee	106	Sycamore	8 N	.25	26.50	.02	
Robert Wright	Patrick	in fee	50	waters Smiths River	7 N	1.00	50.00	.04	

Appendix: Patrick County, Virginia, 1837 Land Tax List:

Name of the Owner [cont'd from prior page]	Explanation of Alterations during the last Year &c	Identification
Sarah Wright Same		Sarah (____) Wright, wife of 1809 Robert Wright of Patrick County, a son of ____ Wright and Mary (____) Wright
Reubin Wright		1872 Reuben Wright of Patrick County, son of 1809 Robert Wright of Patrick County and grandson of ____ Wright and Mary (____) Wright
James T Wright		1875 James Tidwell Wright of Randolph County, Alabama, son of 1847 Robert Wright of Patrick County, grandson of 1811 William Wright of Pittsylvania County, and great grandson of 1755 John Wright of Lunenburg County
Hyram D Wright		1887 Hiram D. Wright of Patrick County, son of 1847 Robert Wright of Patrick County, grandson of 1811 William Wright of Pittsylvania County, and great grandson of 1755 John Wright of Lunenburg County
Robert Wright		1847 Robert Wright of Patrick County, son of 1811 William Wright of Pittsylvania County and grandson of 1755 John Wright of Lunenburg County

1838 LAND TAX LIST

PATRICK COUNTY, VIRGINIA

Appendix: Patrick County, Virginia, 1838 Land Tax List:

Name of the Owner	Residence	Estate	No of Acres of Land	Description of the Land	Distance & bearing from the Court House	rate of land p acre in D & Cts.	Total value of the land	Amt of tax 85¢ p $100	Total amt of tax upon the land
Sarah Wright	Patrick	fee	97	Waters Smiths River	20 N	1.00	97.00	.10	
"	"	"	75	" " "	" "	1.00	75.00	.07	
Reubin Wright	Patrick	fee	100	Smith River	20 NE	1.00	100.00	.10	
James T Wright	Patrick	fee	131	goblintown Creek	15 NE	1.05	137.55	.14	
" "	"	"	32½	" "	" "	.50	62.25	.02	
Hiram D Wright	Patrick	fee	112	Sycamore Creek	8 N	.25	28.00	.03	
" "	"	"	43	" "	"	.25	10.75	.01	
Robert Wright	"	fee	50	waters of Smith River	7 N	1.00	50.00	.05	

Appendix: Patrick County, Virginia, 1838 Land Tax List:

Name of the Owner [cont'd from prior page]	Explanation of Alterations during the last Year &c	Identification
Sarah Wright Same		Sarah (_____) Wright, wife of 1809 Robert Wright of Patrick County, a son of _____ Wright and Mary (_____) Wright
Reubin Wright		1872 Reuben Wright of Patrick County, son of 1809 Robert Wright of Patrick County and grandson of _____ Wright and Mary (_____) Wright
James T Wright " "	14 convyd from Archd Oxley conveyd from Tho H Watkins	1875 James Tidwell Wright of Randolph County, Alabama, son of 1847 Robert Wright of Patrick County, grandson of 1811 Williams Wright of Pittsylvania County, and great grandson of 1755 John Wright of Lunenburg County
Hyram D Wright	conveyd from James T Wright 63 acres of this tract conveyd to C Nicholas	1887 Hiram D. Wright of Patrick County, son of 1847 Robert Wright of Patrick County, grandson of 1811 William Wright of Pittsylvania County, and great grandson of 1755 John Wright of Lunenburg County
Robert Wright		1847 Robert Wright of Patrick County, son of 1811 William Wright of Pittsylvania County and grandson of 1755 John Wright of Lunenburg County

1839 LAND TAX LIST

PATRICK COUNTY, VIRGINIA

Appendix: Patrick County, Virginia, 1839 Land Tax List:

Name of the Owner	Residence	Estate	No of Acres of Land	Description of the Land	Distance & bearing from the Court House	rate of land p acre in D & Cts.	Total value of the land	Amt of tax 85¢ p $100	Total amt of tax upon the land
Sarah Wright	Patrick	fee	97	head waters Smith River	20 NE	1.00	97.00	.10	
"	"	"	75	" " "	" "	1.00	75.00	.07	
Reubin Wright	Patrick	fee	100	Smith River	20 NE	1.00	100.00	.11	
James T Wright	Patrick	fee	131	Goblintown Creek	15 NE	1.05	137.55	.14	
" "	"	"	32½	" "	" "	.50	16.25	.02	
Hiram D Wright	Patrick	fee	112	Sycamore Creek	8 N	.25	28.00	.03	
" "	"	"	435	" "	"	.25	108.75	.11	
Robert Wright	"	fee	50	Waters Smith River	17 N	1.00	50.00	.05	

Appendix: Patrick County, Virginia, 1839 Land Tax List:

Name of the Owner [cont'd from prior page]	Explanation of Alterations during the last Year &c	Identification
Sarah Wright Same		Sarah (____) Wright, wife of 1809 Robert Wright of Patrick County, a son of ____ Wright and Mary (____) Wright
Reubin Wright		1872 Reuben Wright of Patrick County, son of 1809 Robert Wright of Patrick County and grandson of ____ Wright and Mary (____) Wright
James T Wright " "		1875 James Tidwell Wright of Randolph County, Alabama, son of 1847 Robert Wright of Patrick County, grandson of 1811 William Wright of Pittsylvania County, and great grandson of 1755 John Wright of Lunenburg County
Hiram D Wright		1887 Hiram D. Wright of Patrick County, son of 1847 Robert Wright of Patrick County, grandson of 1811 William Wright of Pittsylvania County, and great grandson of 1755 John Wright of Lunenburg County
Robert Wright		1847 Robert Wright of Patrick County, son of 1811 William Wright of Pittsylvania County and grandson of 1755 John Wright of Lunenburg County

1840 LAND TAX LIST

PATRICK COUNTY, VIRGINIA

Appendix: Patrick County, Virginia, 1840 Land Tax List:

Name of the Owner	Residence	Estate	No of Acres of Land	Description of the Land	Distance & bearing from the Court House	rate of land p acre in D & Cts.	Total value of the land	Amt of tax 85¢ p $100	Total amt of tax upon the land
Sally Wright	Patrick	fee	97	Smith River	20 NE	.75	72.75	.07	
"	"	"	75	" "	" "	2.65	198.75	.20	
"	"	"	60	Puppy Creek	__ NE	1.00	.60	.06	
James T Wright	Patrick	fee	131	Goblintown Creek	15 NE	1.35	176.85	.18	
" "	"	"	32½	" "	" "	1.75	56.87½	.06	
Hyram D. Wright	Patrick	fee	112	Sycamore Creek	8 N	.50	56.00	.06	
" "	"	"	43	" "	"	.25	10.75	.01	
Robert Wright	Patrick	fee	50	Sycamore Creek	7 N	1.00	50.00	.05	
Reubin Wright	Patrick	fee	100	Waters Smiths R	20 NE	.75	75.00	.08	

Appendix: Patrick County, Virginia, 1840 Land Tax List:

Name of the Owner [cont'd from prior page]	Explanation of Alterations during the last Year &c	Identification
Sally Wright " "	 Transferred from Gabriel Dehart Sr. by Deed	Sarah (____) Wright, wife of 1809 Robert Wright of Patrick County, a son of ____ Wright and Mary (____) Wright
James T Wright " ".		1875 James Tidwell Wright of Randolph County, Alabama, son of 1847 Robert Wright of Patrick County, grandson of 1811 William Wright of Pittsylvania County, and great grandson of 1755 John Wright of Lunenburg County
Hyram D Wright	This tract changed from 435 are in for motion Received from the owner of Error	1887 Hiram D. Wright of Patrick County, son of 1847 Robert Wright of Patrick County, grandson of 1811 William Wright of Pittsylvania County, and great grandson of 1755 John Wright of Lunenburg County
Robert Wright		1847 Robert Wright of Patrick County, son of 1811 William Wright of Pittsylvania County and grandson of 1755 John Wright of Lunenburg County
Reuben Wright		1872 Reuben Wright of Patrick County, son of 1809 Robert Wright of Patrick County and grandson of ____ Wright and Mary (____) Wright

1841 LAND TAX LIST

PATRICK COUNTY, VIRGINIA

Appendix: Patrick County, Virginia, 1841 Land Tax List:

Name of the Owner	Residence	Estate	No of Acres of Land	Description of the Land	Distance & bearing from the Court House	rate of land p acre in D & Cts.	Total value of the land	Amt of tax 85¢ p $100	Total amt of tax upon the land
Sally Wright	Patrick	fee	97	Smith River	20 NE	.75	72.75	.09	
"	"	"	75	" "	" "	2.65	198.75	.25	
"	"	"	60	Puppy Creek	20 NE	1.00	60.00	.07½	
James T Wright	Patrick	fee	131	Goblintown Creek	15 NE	1.35	176.85	.22	
" "	"	"	32½	" "	" "	1.75	56.87½	.07	
Hyram D. Wright	Patrick	fee	112	Sycamore Creek	8 N	.50	56.00	.07	
" "	"	"	43	" "	"	.25	10.75	.01¼	
" "	"	"	50	" "	"	1.00	50.00	.06¼	
Reubin Wright	Patrick	fee	100	Waters Smiths Creek	20 NE	.75	75.00	.09	

Appendix: Patrick County, Virginia, 1841 Land Tax List:

Name of the Owner [cont'd from prior page]	Explanation of Alterations during the last Year &c	Identification
Sally Wright		Sarah (____) Wright, wife of 1809 Robert Wright of Patrick County, a son of ____ Wright and Mary (____) Wright
"		
"	Transferred from Gabriel Degartz Sr. by Decd	
James T Wright		1875 James Tidwell Wright of Randolph County, son of 1847 Robert Wright of Patrick County Wright of Pittsylvania County, grandson of 1811 William Wright of Pittsylvania County, and great grandson of 1755 John Wright of Lunenburg County
" "		
Hyram D Wright	Transfered from Robert Wright by Deed	1887 Hiram D. Wright of Patrick County, son of 1847 Robert Wright of Patrick County, grandson of 1811 William Wright of Pittsylvania County, and great grandson of 1755 John Wright of Lunenburg County
Reuben Wright		1872 Reuben Wright of Patrick County, son of 1809 Robert Wright of Patrick County and grandson of ____ Wright and Mary (____) Wright

1842 LAND TAX LIST

PATRICK COUNTY, VIRGINIA

Appendix: Patrick County, Virginia, 1842 Land Tax List:

Names of owners	Residence	kind of Estate	No of Acres	Description of the Land	Distance and bearing from the C House	Rate of land per acre	Total value of Land	Aount of Tax on land at 12½¢ pr $100 acre
James T Wright	Patrick	fee	131	Goblintown Creek	15 NE	1.35	176.85	.22
" "	"	"	32½	" "	" "	1.75	56.87½	.07
Hiram D Wright	Patrick	fee	112	Sycamore Creek	8 N	.50	56.00	.07
" "	"	"	43	" "	"	.25	10.75	.01¼
" "	"	"	50	" "	"	1.00	50.00	.06¼
Reuben Wright	Patrick	fee	100	Waters Smiths River	20 NE	.75	75.00	.09
"	"	"	97	" " "	" "	.75	72.75	.09

Appendix: Patrick County, Virginia, 1842 Land Tax List:

Name of owners [cont'd from prior page]	Explanation of Alterations during the preceding year	Identification
James T Wright " "		1875 James Tidwell Wright of Randolph County, Alabama, son of 1847 Robert Wright of Patrick County, grandson of 1811 William Wright of Pittsylvania County, and great grandson of 1755 John Wright of Lunenburg County
Hiram D Wright		1887 Hiram D. Wright of Patrick County, son of 1847 Robert Wright of Patrick County, grandson of 1811 William Wright of Pittsylvania County, and great grandson of 1755 John Wright of Lunenburg County
Reuben Wright	Transferred from Sarah Wright	1872 Reuben Wright of Patrick County, son of 1809 Robert Wright of Patrick County and grandson of ____ Wright and Mary (____) Wright

1843 LAND TAX LIST

PATRICK COUNTY, VIRGINIA

Appendix: Patrick County, Virginia, 1843 Land Tax List:

Names of owners	Residence	kind of Estate	No of Acres	Description of the Land	Distance and bearing from the C House	Rate of land per acre	Total value of Land	Aount of Tax on land at 12½¢ pr $100 acre
Hiram D Wright	Patrick	fee	112	Sycamore creek	8 N	.50	56.00	.08¼
" "	"	"	43	" "	"	.25	10.75	.01¾
" "	"	"	50	" "	"	1.00	50.00	.07½
Reuben Wright	Patrick	fee	100	Waters Smiths River	20 NE	.75	75.00	.11½
"	"	"	97	" " "	" "	.75	72.75	.11¼

Appendix: Patrick County, Virginia, 1843 Land Tax List:

Name of owners [cont'd from prior page]	Explanation of Alterations during the preceding year	Identification
Hiram D Wright	Two tracts in the name of James T Wright transferd to Marshal Ward	1887 Hiram D. Wright of Patrick County, son of 1847 Robert Wright of Patrick County, grandson of 1811 William Wright of Pittsylvania County, and great grandson of 1755 John Wright of Lunenburg County
Reuben Wright		1872 Reuben Wright of Patrick County, son of 1809 Robert Wright of Patrick County and grandson of _____ Wright and Mary (_____) Wright

1844 LAND TAX LIST

PATRICK COUNTY, VIRGINIA

Appendix: Patrick County, Virginia, 1844 Land Tax List:

Names of owners	Residence	kind of Estate	No of Acres	Description of the Land	Distance and bearing from the C House	Rate of land per acre	Total value of Land	Aount of Tax on land at 12½¢ pr $100 acre
Hiram D Wright	Patrick	Fee	112	Waters Sycamore Creek	8 N	.50	56.00	.07¼
" "	"	"	43	" "	"	.25	10.75	.01¼
Reuben Wright	Patrick	Fee	100	Waters Smiths River	20 NE	.75	75.00	.07½
"	"	"	97	" " "	" "	.75	72.75	.09
Robert Wright	Patrick	Fee	50	Sycamore Creek	7 N.	1.00	50.00	.06¼

Appendix: Patrick County, Virginia, 1844 Land Tax List:

Name of owners [cont'd from prior page]	Explanation of Alterations during the preceding year	Identification
Hiram D Wright	50 Acres in the name of Hyram D Wright transferred to Robert Wright by Deed 1844	1887 Hiram D. Wright of Patrick County, son of 1847 Robert Wright of Patrick County, grandson of 1811 William Wright of Pittsylvania County, and great grandson of 1755 John Wright of Lunenburg County
Reuben Wright		1872 Reuben Wright of Patrick County, son of 1809 Robert Wright of Patrick County and grandson of ____ Wright and Mary (____) Wright
Robert Wright	Transferred from Hyram D Wright by Deed 1844	1847 Robert Wright of Patrick County, son of 1811 William Wright of Pittsylvania and grandson of 1755 John Wright of Lunenburg County

1845 LAND TAX LIST

PATRICK COUNTY, VIRGINIA

Appendix: Patrick County, Virginia, 1845 Land Tax List:

Name of Owner.	Residence.	Estate, whether held in fee simple, for life, &c.	No. of Acres.	Description of the land, as to watercourses, mountains and contiguous tracts.	Distance and bearing from the courthouse.	Value of land per acre, including buildings	Sum added to the land on account of buildings.	Total value of the land and buildings.
Hyram D. Wright	Patrick	Fee	112	Waters Sycamore Creek	8 N	.50		56.00
" "	"	"	43	" "	"	.25		10.75
Reuben Wright	Patrick	Fee	100	Waters Smiths River	20 NE	.75		75.00
"	"	"	97	" " "	" "	.75		72.75
Robert Wright	Patrick	Fee	50	Sycamore Creek	7 N.	1.00		50.00

Appendix: Patrick County, Virginia, 1845 Land Tax List:

Name of Owner [cont'd from prior page]	Am't of tax on the whole tract, at the legal rate	Explanation of alterations during the preceding year, especially from whom transferred.	Identification
Hyram D. Wright	.05½ .01		1887 Hiram D. Wright of Patrick County, son of 1847 Robert Wright of Patrick County, grandson of 1811 William Wright of Pittsylvania County, and great grandson of 1755 John Wright of Lunenburg County
Reuben Wright	.07½ .07¼		1872 Reuben Wright of Patrick County, son of 1809 Robert Wright of Patrick County and grandson of _____ Wright and Mary (_____) Wright
Robert Wright	.05		1847 Robert Wright of Patrick County, son of 1811 William Wright of Pittsylvania County and grandson of 1755 John Wright of Lunenburg County

1846 LAND TAX LIST

PATRICK COUNTY, VIRGINIA

Appendix: Patrick County, Virginia, 1846 Land Tax List:

Name of Owner.	Residence.	Estate, whether held in fee simple, for life, &c.	No. of Acres.	Description of the land, as to watercourses, mountains and contiguous tracts.	Distance and bearing from the courthouse.	Value of land per acre, including buildings	Sum added to the land on account of buildings.	Total value of the land and buildings.
Hiram D. Wright	Patrick	Fee	112	waters Sycamore Creek	8 N	.50		56.00
" "	"	"	43	" "	"	.25		10.75
Reuben Wright	Patrick	Fee	100	Smiths River	20 NE	.75		75.00
"	"	"	97	" "	" "	.75		72.75
Robert Wright	Patrick	Fee	50	Sycamore Creek	7 N.	1.00		50.00

Appendix: Patrick County, Virginia, 1846 Land Tax List:

Name of Owner [cont'd from prior page]	Am't of tax on the whole tract, at the legal rate	Explanation of alterations during the preceding year, especially from whom transferred.	Identification
Hiram D. Wright	.05½ .01		1887 Hiram D. Wright of Patrick County, son of 1847 Robert Wright of Patrick County, grandson of 1811 William Wright of Pittsylvania County, and great grandson of 1755 John Wright of Lunenburg County
Reuben Wright	.07½ .07¼		1872 Reuben Wright of Patrick County, son of 1809 Robert Wright of Patrick County and grandson of _____ Wright and Mary (_____) Wright
Robert Wright	.05		1847 Robert Wright of Patrick County, son of 1811 William Wright of Pittsylvania County and grandson of 1755 John Wright of Lunenburg County

1847 LAND TAX LIST

PATRICK COUNTY, VIRGINIA

Appendix: Patrick County, Virginia, 1847 Land Tax List:

Name of Owner.	Residence.	Estate, whether held in fee simple, for life, &c.	No. of Acres.	Description of the land, as to watercourses, mountains and contiguous tracts.	Distance and bearing from the courthouse.	Value of land per acre, including buildings	Sum added to the land on account of buildings.	Total value of the land and buildings.
Hiram D. Wright	Patrick	Fee	112	waters Sycamore Creek	8 N	.50		56.00
" "	"	"	43	" "	"	.25		10.75
Reuben Wright	Patrick	Fee	100	Smiths River	20 NE	.75		75.00
"	"	"	97	" "	" "	.75		72.75
Robert Wright Decd	Patrick	Fee	50	Sycamore Creek	7 N.	1.00		50.00
Jubal Wright	Patrick	Fee	100	Smiths River	20 NE	1.00		100.00

Appendix: Patrick County, Virginia, 1847 Land Tax List:

Name of Owner [cont'd from prior page]	Am't of tax on the whole tract, at the legal rate	Explanation of alterations during the preceding year, especially from whom transferred.	Identification
Hiram D. Wright	.05½ .01		1887 Hiram D. Wright of Patrick County, son of 1847 Robert Wright of Patrick County, grandson of 1811 William Wright of Pittsylvania County, and great grandson of 1755 John Wright of Lunenburg County
Reuben Wright	.07½ .07		1872 Reuben Wright of Patrick County, son of 1809 Robert Wright of Patrick County and grandson of _____ Wright and Mary (_____) Wright
Robert Wright Decd	.05		1847 Robert Wright of Patrick County, son of 1811 William Wright of Pittsylvania County and grandson of 1755 John Wright of Lunenburg County
Jubal Wright	.10		1868 Jubal Wright of Patrick County, son of John N. Wright, grandson of 1809 Robert Wright of Patrick County, and great grandson of _____ Wright and Mary (_____) Wright

1848 LAND TAX LIST

PATRICK COUNTY, VIRGINIA

Appendix: Patrick County, Virginia, 1848 Land Tax List:

List A:

Name of Owner.	Residence.	Estate, whether held in fee simple, for life, &c.	No. of Acres.	Description of the land, as to watercourses, mountains and contiguous tracts.	Distance and bearing from the courthouse.	Value of land per acre, including buildings	Sum added to the land on account of buildings.	Total value of the land and buildings.
Hiram D. Wright	Patrick	Fee	112	Waters Sycamore	8 N	.50		56.00
" "	"	"	43	" "	"	.25		10.75
Reuben Wright	Patrick	Fee	100	Smiths River	20 NE	.75		75.00
"	"	"	97	" "	" "	.75		72.75
Robert Wright Decd	Patrick	Fee	50	Sycamore Creek	7 N.	1.00		50.00

Appendix: Patrick County, Virginia, 1848 Land Tax List:

List A:

Name of Owner [cont'd from prior page]	Am't of tax on the whole tract, at the legal rate	Explanation of alterations during the preceding year, especially from whom transferred.	Identification
Hiram D. Wright	.05½ .01		1887 Hiram D. Wright of Patrick County, son of 1847 Robert Wright of Patrick County, grandson of 1811 William Wright of Pittsylvania County, and great grandson of 1755 John Wright of Lunenburg County
Reuben Wright	.07½ .07		1872 Reuben Wright of Patrick County, son of 1809 Robert Wright of Patrick County and grandson of _____ Wright and Mary (_____) Wright
Robert Wright Decd	.05		1847 Robert Wright of Patrick County, son of 1811 William Wright of Pittsylvania County and grandson of 1755 John Wright of Lunenburg County

1849 LAND TAX LIST

PATRICK COUNTY, VIRGINIA

Appendix: Patrick County, Virginia, 1849 Land Tax List:

List A:

Name of Owner.	Residence.	Estate, whether held in fee simple, for life, &c.	No. of Acres.	Description of the land, as to watercourses, mountains and contiguous tracts.	Distance and bearing from the courthouse.	Value of land per acre, including buildings	Sum added to the land on account of buildings.	Total value of the land and buildings.
Hiram D. Wright	Patrick	Fee	112	Waters Sycamore	8 N	.50		56.00
" "	"	"	43	" "	"	.25		10.75
Reuben Wright	Patrick	Fee	100	Smiths River	20 NE	.75		75.00
"	"	"	97	" "	" "	.75		72.75
Robert Wright Decd	Patrick	Fee	50	Sycamore Creek	7 N.	1.00		50.00
Jubal Wright	Patrick	Fee	100	Smiths River	20 NE	1.00		100.00

Appendix: Patrick County, Virginia, 1849 Land Tax List:

List A:

Name of Owner [cont'd from prior page]	Am't of tax on the whole tract, at the legal rate	Explanation of alterations during the preceding year, especially from whom transferred.	Identification
Hiram D. Wright	.06	The Wilks Transfered to N Pet	1887 Hiram D. Wright of Patrick County, son of 1847 Robert Wright of Patrick County, grandson of 1811 William Wright of Pittsylvania County, and great grandson of 1755 John Wright of Lunenburg County
	.01	S. H. Wood in Franklin	
Reuben Wright County	.08		1872 Reuben Wright of Patrick County, son of 1809 Robert Wright of Patrick and grandson of _____ Wright and Mary (_____) Wright
	.07		
	.02	Transfered from H. Crumb	
Robert Wright Decd	.05		1847 Robert Wright of Patrick County, son of 1811 William Wright of Pittsylvania County and grandson of 1755 John Wright of Lunenburg County
Jubal Wright	.10		1868 Jubal Wright of Patrick County, son of John N. Wright, grandson of 1809 Robert Wright of Patrick County, and great grandson of _____ Wright and Mary (_____) Wright

Appendix: Patrick County, Virginia, 1849 Land Tax List:

List B:

Name of Owner.	Residence.	Estate, whether held in fee simple, for life, &c.	No. of Acres.	Description of the land, as to watercourses, mountains and contiguous tracts.	Distance and bearing from the courthouse.	Value of land per acre, including buildings	Sum added to the land on account of buildings.	Total value of the land and buildings.
Josiah Wright	Patrick	Fee	101	W N mayo	14 NE	1.00		101.00

Appendix: Patrick County, Virginia, 1849 Land Tax List:

List B:

Name of Owner [cont'd from prior page]	Am't of tax on the whole tract, at the legal rate	Explanation of alterations during the preceding year, especially from whom transferred.	Identification
Josiah Wright	.10	Transfered from Abram Spencer	1862 Josiah Wright of Patrick County, son of John N. Wright, grandson of 1809 Robert Wright of Patrick County, and great grandson of ____ Wright and Mary (____) Wright

1850 LAND TAX LIST

PATRICK COUNTY, VIRGINIA

Appendix: Patrick County, Virginia, 1850 Land Tax List:

List A:

Name of Owner.	Residence.	Estate, whether held in fee simple, for life, &c.	No. of Acres.	Description of the land, as to watercourses, mountains and contiguous tracts.	Distance and bearing from the courthouse.	Value of land per acre, including buildings	Sum added to the land on account of buildings.	Total value of the land and buildings.
Hiram D Wright	Patrick	Fee	112	waters Sycamore	8 N	.50		56.00
" "	"	"	43	" "	"	.25		10.75
Reuben Wright	Patrick	Fee	100	Smiths River	20 NE	.75		75.00
" "	"	"	97	" "	"	.75		72.75
" "	"	"	9½	" "	"	2.65		24.17½
Robert Wright decd	Patrick	Fee	50	Sycamore C	7 N	1.00		50.00
Jubal Wright	Patrick	Fee	100	Smiths River	20 NE	1.00		100.00

Appendix: Patrick County, Virginia, 1850 Land Tax List:

List A:

Name of Owner [cont'd from prior page]	Am't of tax on the whole tract, at the legal rate	Explanation of alterations during the preceding year, especially from whom transferred.	Identification
Hiram D Wright	.06		1887 Hiram D. Wright of Patrick County, son of 1847 Robert Wright of Patrick County, grandson of 1811 William Wright of Pittsylvania County, and great grandson of 1755 John Wright of Lunenburg County
" "	.01		
Reuben Wright	.08		1872 Reuben Wright of Patrick County, son of 1809 Robert Wright of Patrick County and grandson of ____ Wright and Mary (____) Wright
" "	.07		
" "	.02		
Robert Wright decd	.05		1847 Robert Wright of Patrick County, son of 1811 William Wright of Pittsylvania County and grandson of 1755 John Wright of Lunenburg County
Jubal Wright	.10		1868 Jubal Wright of Patrick County, son of John N. Wright, grandson of 1809 Robert Wright of Patrick County, and great grandson of ____ Wright and Mary (____) Wright

Appendix: Patrick County, Virginia, 1850 Land Tax List:

List B:

Name of Owner.	Residence.	Estate, whether held in fee simple, for life, &c.	No. of Acres.	Description of the land, as to watercourses, mountains and contiguous tracts.	Distance and bearing from the courthouse.	Value of land per acre, including buildings	Sum added to the land on account of buildings.	Total value of the land and buildings.
Josiah Wright	Patrick	Fee	101	W N Mayo	14 NE	1.00		101.00

Appendix: Patrick County, Virginia, 1850 Land Tax List:

List B:

Name of Owner [cont'd from prior page]	Am't of tax on the whole tract, at the legal rate	Explanation of alterations during the preceding year, especially from whom transferred.	Identification
Josiah Wright	.10		1862 Josiah Wright of Patrick County, son of John N. Wright, grandson of 1809 Robert Wright of Patrick County, and great grandson of _____ Wright and Mary (_____) Wright

1851 LAND TAX LIST

PATRICK COUNTY, VIRGINIA

Appendix: Patrick County, Virginia, 1851 Land Tax List:

District of F. G. Smith:

Name of Owner.	Residence.	Estate, whether held in fee simple, for life, &c.	No. of Acres.	Name of Tract	Description of the land, as to watercourses, mountains and contiguous tracts.	Distance and bearing from the courthouse.	Value of land per acre, including buildings
Josiah Wright	Patrick	Fee	101		Ws of N. Mayo	14 N.E.	2.00

Appendix: Patrick County, Virginia, 1851 Land Tax List:

District of F. G. Smith:

Name of Owner [cont'd from prior page]	Sum added to the land on account of buildings	Total value of the land and buildings	Am't of tax on the whole tract, at the legal rate	Amount of tax for county purposes	Explanation of alterations during the preceding year, especially from whom transferred.	Identification
Josiah Wright		202.00	.24			1862 Josiah Wright of Patrick County, son of John N. Wright, grandson of 1809 Robert Wright of Patrick County, and great grandson of ____ Wright and Mary (____) Wright

Appendix: Patrick County, Virginia, 1851 Land Tax List:

District of C. Ross:

Name of Owner.	Residence.	Estate, whether held in fee simple, for life, &c.	No. of Acres.	Name of Tract	Description of the land, as to watercourses, mountains and contiguous tracts.	Distance and bearing from the courthouse.	Value of land per acre, including buildings
Hiram D. Wright	Patrick	Fee	112		W. Syc C	7 N	1.50
" "	"	"	43		" "	"	1.00
Robt Wright Decd	Patrick	Fee	50		B "	7 N	2.00
Jubal Wright	Patrick	Fee	100		S. River	20 NE	2.50
Reuben Wright	Pat	Fee	100		Smiths River	20 NE	2.00
" "	"	"	97		" "	"	1.00
" "	"	"	9½		" "	"	1.05

Appendix: Patrick County, Virginia, 1851 Land Tax List:

District of C. Ross:

Name of Owner [cont'd from prior page]	Sum added to the land on account of buildings	Total value of the land and buildings	Am't of tax on the whole tract, at the legal rate	Amount of tax for county purposes	Explanation of alterations during the preceding year, especially from whom transferred.	Identification
Hiram D. Wright " "		168.00 46.00	.20 .05			1887 Hiram D. Wright of Patrick County, son of 1847 Robert Wright of Patrick County, grandson of 1811 William Wright of Pittsylvania County, and great grandson of 1755 John Wright of Lunenburg County
Robt Wright Decd		100.00	.12			1847 Robert Wright of Patrick County, son of 1811 William Wright of Pittsylvania County and grandson of 1755 John Wright of Lunenburg County
Jubal Wright		250.00	.30			1868 Jubal Wright of Patrick County, son of John N. Wright, grandson of 1809 Robert Wright of Patrick County, and great grandson of ____ Wright and Mary (____) Wright
Reuben Wright " " " "		200.00 97.00 10.00	.24 .12 .01			1872 Reuben Wright of Patrick County, son of 1809 Robert Wright of Patrick County and grandson of ____ Wright and Mary (____) Wright

1852 LAND TAX LIST

PATRICK COUNTY, VIRGINIA

Appendix: Patrick County, Virginia, 1852 Land Tax List:

District of F. G. Smith:

Name of Owner.	Residence.	Estate, whether held in fee simple, for life, &c.	No. of Acres.	Name of Tract	Description of the land, as to watercourses, mountains and contiguous tracts.	Distance and bearing from the courthouse.	Value of land per acre, including buildings
Josiah Wright	Patrick	Fee	101		W of N. Mayo	14 N.E.	2.00

Appendix: Patrick County, Virginia, 1852 Land Tax List:

District of F. G. Smith:

Name of Owner [cont'd from prior page]	Sum added to the land on account of buildings	Total value of the land and buildings	Am't of tax on the whole tract, at the legal rate	Amount of tax for county purposes	Explanation of alterations during the preceding year, especially from whom transferred.	Identification
Josiah Wright		202.00	.36			1862 Josiah Wright of Patrick County, son of John N. Wright, grandson of 1809 Robert Wright of Patrick County, and great grandson of ____ Wright and Mary (____) Wright

Appendix: Patrick County, Virginia, 1852 Land Tax List:

District of C. Ross:

Name of Owner.	Residence.	Estate, whether held in fee simple, for life, &c.	No. of Acres.	Name of Tract	Description of the land, as to watercourses, mountains and contiguous tracts.	Distance and bearing from the courthouse.	Value of land per acre, including buildings
Hiram D. Wright	Patrick	Fee	112		waters Sycamore Cr	7 N	1.50
" "	"	"	43		" "	"	1.00
Robt Wright Decd	Patrick	Fee	50		waters Sycamore Cr	7 N	2.00
Jubal Wright	Patrick	Fee	100		Smiths river	22 NE	7.50
" "	"	"	130		Both sides Smiths river	20 "	1.00
Reuben Wright	Patrick	Fee	100		Smiths River	20 NE	2.00
" "	"	"	97		" "	"	1.00
" "	"	"	9½		" "	"	1.05

Appendix: Patrick County, Virginia, 1852 Land Tax List:

District of C. Ross:

Name of Owner [cont'd from prior page]	Sum added to the land on account of buildings	Total value of the land and buildings	Am't of tax on the whole tract, at the legal rate	Amount of tax for county purposes	Explanation of alterations during the preceding year, especially from whom transferred.	Identification
Hiram D. Wright		168.00	.20			1887 Hiram D. Wright of Patrick County, son of 1847 Robert Wright of Patrick County, grandson of 1811 William Wright of Pittsylvania County, and great grandson of 1755 John Wright of Lunenburg County
" "		43.00	.08			
Robt Wright Decd		100.00	.18			1847 Robert Wright of Patrick County, son of 1811 William Wright of Pittsylvania County and grandson of 1755 John Wright of Lunenburg County
Jubal Wright		250.00	.45			1868 Jubal Wright of Patrick County, son of John N. Wright, grandson of 1809 Robert Wright of Patrick County, and great grandson of ____ Wright and Mary (____) Wright
" "		130.00	.23		New grant	
Reuben Wright		200.00	.36			1872 Reuben Wright of Patrick County, son of 1809 Robert Wright of Patrick County and grandson of ____ Wright and Mary (____) Wright
" "		97.00	.18			
" "		10.00	.02			

1853 LAND TAX LIST

PATRICK COUNTY, VIRGINIA

Appendix: Patrick County, Virginia, 1853 Land Tax List:

District of John G. Tatum:

Name of Owner.	Residence.	Estate, whether held in fee simple, for life, &c.	No. of Acres.	Name of Tract	Description of the land, as to watercourses, mountains and contiguous tracts.	Distance and bearing from the courthouse.	Value of land per acre, including buildings
Josiah Wright	Patrick	Fee	101		waters of North Mayo	14 N.E.	2.00

Appendix: Patrick County, Virginia, 1852 Land Tax List:

District of John G. Tatum:

Name of Owner [cont'd from prior page]	Sum added to the land on account of buildings	Total value of the land and buildings	Am't of tax on the whole tract, at the legal rate	Amount of tax for county purposes	Explanation of alterations during the preceding year, especially from whom transferred.	Identification
Josiah Wright		202.00	.41			1862 Josiah Wright of Patrick County, son of John N. Wright, grandson of 1809 Robert Wright of Patrick County, and great grandson of ____ Wright and Mary (____) Wright

Appendix: Patrick County, Virginia, 1853 Land Tax List:

District of C. Ross:

Name of Owner.	Residence.	Estate, whether held in fee simple, for life, &c.	No. of Acres.	Name of Tract	Description of the land, as to watercourses, mountains and contiguous tracts.	Distance and bearing from the courthouse.	Value of land per acre, including buildings
Hiram D. Wright	Patrick	Fee	112		ws Sycamore Cr	7 N	1.50
" "	"	"	43		" "	"	1.00
Robt Wright Decd	Patrick	Fee	50		ws Sycamore Cr	7 N	2.00
Jubal Wright	Patrick	Fee	100		Smiths river	22 NE	2.50
" "	"	"	130		Both sides Do	20 "	1.00
Reuben Wright	Pat	Fee	100		Smiths River	20 NE	2.00
" "	"	"	97		" "	"	1.00
" "	"	"	9½		" "	"	1.05

Appendix: Patrick County, Virginia, 1853 Land Tax List:

District of C. Ross:

Name of Owner [cont'd from prior page]	Sum added to the land on account of buildings	Total value of the land and buildings	Am't of tax on the whole tract, at the legal rate	Amount of tax for county purposes	Explanation of alterations during the preceding year, especially from whom transferred.	Identification
Hiram D. Wright " "		168.00 43.00	.34 .09			1887 Hiram D. Wright of Patrick County, son of 1847 Robert Wright of Patrick County, grandson of 1811 William Wright of Pittsylvania County, and great grandson of 1755 John Wright of Lunenburg County
Robt Wright Decd		100.00	.20			1847 Robert Wright of Patrick County, son of 1811 William Wright of Pittsylvania County and grandson of 1755 John Wright of Lunenburg County
Jubal Wright " "		250.00 130.00	.50 .26			1868 Jubal Wright of Patrick County, son of John N. Wright, grandson of 1809 Robert Wright of Patrick County, and great grandson of ____ Wright and Mary (____) Wright
Reuben Wright " " " "		200.00 97.00 10.00	.40 .20 .03			1872 Reuben Wright of Patrick County, son of 1809 Robert Wright of Patrick County and grandson of ____ Wright and Mary (____) Wright

1854 LAND TAX LIST

PATRICK COUNTY, VIRGINIA

Appendix: Patrick County, Virginia, 1854 Land Tax List:

District of John G. Tatum:

Name of Owner.	Residence.	Estate, whether held in fee simple, for life, &c.	No. of Acres.	Name of Tract	Description of the land, as to watercourses, mountains and contiguous tracts.	Distance and bearing from the courthouse.	Value of land per acre, including buildings
Josiah Wright	Patrick	Fee	101		Waters N Mayo	16 N.E.	2.00

Appendix: Patrick County, Virginia, 1854 Land Tax List:

District of John G. Tatum:

Name of Owner [cont'd from prior page]	Sum added to the land on account of buildings	Total value of the land and buildings	Am't of tax on the whole tract, at the legal rate	Amount of tax for county purposes	Explanation of alterations during the preceding year, especially from whom transferred.	Identification
Josiah Wright		202.00	.40			1862 Josiah Wright of Patrick County, son of John N. Wright, grandson of 1809 Robert Wright of Patrick County, and great grandson of ____ Wright and Mary (____) Wright

Appendix: Patrick County, Virginia, 1854 Land Tax List:

District of C. Ross:

Name of Owner.	Residence.	Estate, whether held in fee simple, for life, &c.	No. of Acres.	Name of Tract	Description of the land, as to watercourses, mountains and contiguous tracts.	Distance and bearing from the courthouse.	Value of land per acre, including buildings
Hiram D. Wright	Patrick	Fee	112		ws Sycamore Cr	7 N	1.50
" "	"	"	43		" "	"	1.00
Robt Wright Decd	Patrick	Fee	50		ws Sycamore Cr	7 N	2.00
Jubal Wright	Patrick	Fee	100		Smiths river	22 NE	2.50
" "	"	"	130		both sides Smiths River	20 "	1.00
Reuben Wright	Pat	Fee	100		Smiths river	20 NE	2.00
" "	"	"	97		" "	"	1.00
" "	"	"	9½		" "	"	1.05

Appendix: Patrick County, Virginia, 1854 Land Tax List:

District of C. Ross:

Name of Owner [cont'd from prior page]	Sum added to the land on account of buildings	Total value of the land and buildings	Am't of tax on the whole tract, at the legal rate	Amount of tax for county purposes	Explanation of alterations during the preceding year, especially from whom transferred.	Identification
Hiram D. Wright " "		168.00 43.00	.34 .09			1887 Hiram D. Wright of Patrick County, son of 1847 Robert Wright of Patrick County, grandson of 1811 William Wright of Pittsylvania County, and great grandson of 1755 John Wright of Lunenburg County
Robt Wright Decd		100.00	.20			1847 Robert Wright of Patrick County, son of 1811 William Wright of Pittsylvania County and grandson of 1755 John Wright of Lunenburg County
Jubal Wright " "		250.00 130.00	.50 .26			1868 Jubal Wright of Patrick County, son of John N. Wright, grandson of 1809 Robert Wright of Patrick County, and great grandson of ____ Wright and Mary (____) Wright
Reuben Wright " " " "		200.00 97.00 10.00	.40 .20 .02			1872 Reuben Wright of Patrick County, son of 1809 Robert Wright of Patrick County and grandson of ____ Wright and Mary (____) Wright

1855 LAND TAX LIST

PATRICK COUNTY, VIRGINIA

Appendix: Patrick County, Virginia, 1855 Land Tax List:

District of C. Ross:

Name of Owner.	Residence.	Estate, whether held in fee simple, for life, &c.	No. of Acres.	Name of Tract	Description of the land, as to watercourses, mountains and contiguous tracts.	Distance and bearing from the courthouse.	Value of land per acre, including buildings
Hiram D. Wright	Patrick	Fee	112	No Name	Ws Sycamore Cr	7 N	1.50
" "	"	"	43	" "	" "	"	1.00
Robt Wright Decd	Patrick	Fee	50		Ws Sycamore Cr	7 N	2.00
Jubal Wright	Patrick	Fee	100		Smiths river	22 NE	2.50
" "	"	"	130		both sides Smiths River	20 "	1.00
Reuben Wright	Patrick	Fee	100		Smiths river	20 NE	2.00
" "	"	"	97		" "	"	1.00
" "	"	"	9½		" "	"	1.05
" "	"	"	243		" "	"	2.47

Appendix: Patrick County, Virginia, 1855 Land Tax List:

District of C. Ross:

Name of Owner.	Residence.	Estate, whether held in fee simple, for life, &c.	No. of Acres.	Name of Tract	Description of the land, as to watercourses, mountains and contiguous tracts.	Distance and bearing from the courthouse.	Value of land per acre, including buildings
Josiah Wright	Patrick	Fee	101		N Mayo	16 N.E.	2.00

Appendix: Patrick County, Virginia, 1855 Land Tax List:

District of C. Ross:

Name of Owner [cont'd from prior page]	Sum added to the land on account of buildings	Total value of the land and buildings	Am't of tax on the whole tract, at the legal rate	Amount of tax for county purposes	Explanation of alterations during the preceding year, especially from whom transferred.	Identification
Hiram D. Wright " "		168.00 43.00	.34 .09			1887 Hiram D. Wright of Patrick County, son of 1847 Robert Wright of Patrick County, grandson of 1811 William Wright of Pittsylvania County, and great grandson of 1755 John Wright of Lunenburg County
Robt Wright Decd		100.00	.20			1847 Robert Wright of Patrick County, son of 1811 William Wright of Pittsylvania County and grandson of 1755 John Wright of Lunenburg County
Jubal Wright " "		250.00 130.00	.50 .26			1868 Jubal Wright of Patrick County, son of John N. Wright, grandson of 1809 Robert Wright of Patrick County, and great grandson of ____ Wright and Mary (____) Wright
Reuben Wright " " " " " "		200.00 97.00 10.00 600.00	.40 .20 .02 1.26		Transfrd from Henry Crum	1872 Reuben Wright of Patrick County, son of 1809 Robert Wright of Patrick County and grandson of ____ Wright and Mary (____) Wright

Appendix: Patrick County, Virginia, 1855 Land Tax List:

District of C. Ross:

Name of Owner [cont'd from prior page]	Sum added to the land on account of buildings	Total value of the land and buildings	Am't of tax on the whole tract, at the legal rate	Amount of tax for county purposes	Explanation of alterations during the preceding year, especially from whom transferred.	Identification
Josiah Wright		202.00	.46			1862 Josiah Wright of Patrick County, son of John N. Wright, grandson of 1809 Robert Wright of Patrick County, and great grandson of ____ Wright and Mary (____) Wright

1856 LAND TAX LIST

PATRICK COUNTY, VIRGINIA

Appendix: Patrick County, Virginia, 1856 Land Tax List:

District of _____ :

Name of Owner.	Residence.	Estate, whether held in fee simple, for life, &c.	No. of Acres.	Name of Tract	Description of the land, as to watercourses, mountains and contiguous tracts.	Distance and bearing from the courthouse.	Value of land per acre, including buildings
Hiram D. Wright	Patrick	Fee	112	No Name	Ws Sycamore cr	7 N	1.50
" "	"	"	43	" "	" "	"	1.00
Robt Wright Decd	Patrick	Fee	50		Ws Sycamore Cr	7 N	2.00
Jubal Wright	Patrick	Fee	100		Smiths river	22 NE	2.50
" "	"	"	130		both sides Smiths	20 "	1.00
Reuben Wright	Patrick	Fee	100		Smiths R	20 NE	2.00
" "	"	"	97		" "	"	1.00
" "	"	"	9½		" "	"	1.05
" "	"	"	243		" "	"	2.47
Josiah Wright	Patrick	Fee	101		N Mayo	16 E	2.00

Appendix: Patrick County, Virginia, 1856 Land Tax List:

District of C. Ross:

Name of Owner [cont'd from prior page]	Sum added to the land on account of buildings	Total value of the land and buildings	Am't of tax on the whole tract, at the legal rate	Amount of tax for county purposes	Explanation of alterations during the preceding year, especially from whom transferred.	Identification
Hiram D. Wright		168.00	.68			1887 Hiram D. Wright of Patrick County, son of 1847 Robert Wright of Patrick County, grandson of 1811 William Wright of Pittsylvania County, and great grandson of 1755 John Wright of Lunenburg County
" "		43.00	.18			
Robt Wright Decd		100.00	.40			1847 Robert Wright of Patrick County, son of 1811 William Wright of Pittsylvania County and grandson of 1755 John Wright of Lunenburg County
Jubal Wright		250.00	1.00			1868 Jubal Wright of Patrick County, son of John N. Wright, grandson of 1809 Robert Wright of Patrick County, and great grandson of _____ Wright and Mary (____) Wright
" "		130.00	.52			
Reuben Wright		200.00	.80			1872 Reuben Wright of Patrick County, son of 1809 Robert Wright of Patrick County and grandson of _____ Wright and Mary (____) Wright
" "		97.00	.40			
" "		10.00	.04			
" "		600.00	2.46			

Appendix: Patrick County, Virginia, 1856 Land Tax List:

District of C. Ross:

Name of Owner [cont'd from prior page]	Sum added to the land on account of buildings	Total value of the land and buildings	Am't of tax on the whole tract, at the legal rate	Amount of tax for county purposes	Explanation of alterations during the preceding year, especially from whom transferred.	Identification
Josiah Wright		202.00	.80			1862 Josiah Wright of Patrick County, son of John N. Wright, grandson of 1809 Robert Wright of Patrick County, and great grandson of ____ Wright and Mary (____) Wright

1857 LAND TAX LIST

PATRICK COUNTY, VIRGINIA

Appendix: Patrick County, Virginia, 1857 Land Tax List:

District of G. Sondefur:

Name of Owner.	Residence.	Estate, whether held in fee simple, for life, &c.	No. of Acres.	Name of Tract	Description of the land, as to water courses, mountains and contiguous tracts.	Distance and bearing from the courthouse.	Value of land per acre, including buildings
Robt Wright Decd	Patrick	Fee	50	No Name			4.00
Hiram Wright	Patrick	Fee	112	No Name			2.00
" "	"	"	43	" "			2.00
Jubal Wright	Patrick	Fee	100	___ Blue Ridge	Smiths river	22 NE	5.00
" "	"	"	130	" " "	" "	20 "	2.50
Reuben Wright	Patrick	Fee	100	___ Blue Ridge	Smiths river	20 NE	2.00
" "	"	"	97	" " "	" "	"	1.25
" "	"	"	9½	" " "	" "	"	1.00
" "	"	"	243	" " "	" "	"	3.00
Josiah Wright	Patrick	Fee	101		N Mayo River	16 E	4.00

Appendix: Patrick County, Virginia, 1857 Land Tax List:

District of G, Sondefur:

Name of Owner [cont'd from prior page]	Sum added to the land on account of buildings	Total value of the land and buildings	Amount of tax on the whole tract, at the legal rate	Amount of tax for county purposes	Explanation of alterations during the preceding year, especially from whom transferred, and when and how owner derived the land	Identification
Robt Wright Decd	30.00	300.00	.80			1847 Robert Wright of Patrick County, son of 1811 William Wright of Pittsylvania County and grandson of 1755 John Wright of Lunenburg County
Hiram Wright " "	73.00	224.00 86.00	.90 .24			1887 Hiram D. Wright of Patrick County, son of 1847 Robert Wright of Patrick County, grandson of 1811 William Wright of Pittsylvania County, and great grandson of 1755 John Wright of Lunenburg County
Jubal Wright " "	80.00 80.00	500.00 325.00	2.00 1.30			1868 Jubal Wright of Patrick County, son of John N. Wright, grandson of 1809 Robert Wright of Patrick County, and great grandson of ____ Wright and Mary (____) Wright
Reuben Wright " " " " " "	50.00 " " 122.00	200.00 121.00 10.00 727.00	.80 .48 .04 1.92			1872 Reuben Wright of Patrick County, son of 1809 Robert Wright of Patrick County and grandson of ____ Wright and Mary (____) Wright
Josiah Wright	50.00	604.00	.63			1862 Josiah Wright of Patrick County, son of John N. Wright, grandson of 1809 Robert Wright of Patrick County, and great grandson of ____ Wright and Mary (____) Wright

1858 LAND TAX LIST

PATRICK COUNTY, VIRGINIA

Appendix: Patrick County, Virginia, 1858 Land Tax List:

District of G. Sondefur:

Name of Owner.	Residence.	Estate, whether held in fee simple, for life, &c.	No. of Acres.	Name of Tract	Description of the land, as to water courses, mountains and contiguous tracts.	Distance and bearing from the courthouse.	Value of land per acre, including buildings
Robt Wright Decd	Patrick	Fee	50	No Name	Sycamore cr.	7 NE	4.00
Hiram D. Wright	Patrick	Fee	112	No Name	Sycamore cr.	7 NE	2.00
" "	"	"	48	" "	" "	" "	2.00
Jubal Wright	Patrick	Fee	100	Spur Mt.	Smiths Riv	22 NE	5.00
" "	"	"	130	" "	" "	20 "	2.50
" "	"	"	106	" "	Puppy's Cr	18 "	3.22
Reuben Wright	Patrick	Fee	100	Spur Mt.	Puppy's cr.	18 NE	2.00
" "	"	"	97	" "	" "	"	1.25
" "	"	"	9½	" "	" "	"	1.00
" "	"	"	243	" "	" "	"	3.00
Josiah Wright	Patrick	Fee	101		N Mayo	16 E	4.00

Appendix: Patrick County, Virginia, 1858 Land Tax List:

District of G, Sondefur:

Name of Owner [cont'd from prior page]	Sum added to the land on account of buildings	Total value of the land and buildings	Amount of tax on the whole tract, at the legal rate	Amount of tax for county purposes	Explanation of alterations during the preceding year, especially from whom transferred, and when and how owner derived the land	Identification
Robt Wright Decd	30.00	200.00	.80			1847 Robert Wright of Patrick County, son of 1811 William Wright of Pittsylvania County and grandson of 1755 John Wright of Lunenburg County
Hiram D. Wright	75.00	224.00	.90			1887 Hiram D. Wright of Patarick County, son of 1847 Robert Wright of Patrick County, grandson of 1811 William Wright of Pittsylvania County, and great grandson of 1755 John Wright of Lunenburg County
	75.00	86.00	.34			
Jubal Wright	80.00	500.00	2.00			1868 Jubal Wright of Patrick County, son of John N. Wright, grandson of 1809 Robert Wright of Patrick County, and great grandson of ____ Wright and Mary (____) Wright
" "	80.00	325.00	1.30			
" "	85.00	341.00	1.36		Transferd from Jas. D. Martin	
Reuben Wright	50.00	200.00	.80			1872 Reuben Wright of Patrick County, son of 1809 Robert Wright of Patrick County and grandson of ____ Wright and Mary (____) Wright
" "	"	121.00	.48			
" "	"	10.00	.04			
" "	122.00	729.00	2.92			
Josiah Wright	150.00	404.00	1.62			1862 Josiah Wright of Patrick County, son of John N. Wright, grandson of 1809 Robert Wright of Patrick County, and great grandson of ____ Wright and Mary (____) Wright

1859 LAND TAX LIST

PATRICK COUNTY, VIRGINIA

Appendix: Patrick County, Virginia, 1859 Land Tax List:

District of G. Sondefur:

Name of Owner.	Residence.	Estate, whether held in fee simple, for life, &c.	No. of Acres.	Name of Tract	Description of the land, as to water courses, mountains and contiguous tracts.	Distance and bearing from the courthouse.	Value of land per acre, including buildings
Robt Wright Decd	Patrick	Fee	50	No Name	Sycamore	7 NE	4.00
H. D. Wright	Patrick	Fee	112	No Name	Sycamore	7 NE	2.00
"	"	"	44	" "	"	" "	2.00
"	"	"	55	" "	"	" "	3.00
Jubal Wright	Patrick	Fee	100	Spur Mt.	Smiths Riv	22 NE	5.00
" "	"	"	130	" "	" "	20 "	2.50
" "	"	"	106	" "	Puppy cr.	18 "	3.22
Reuben Wright	Patrick	Fee	100	Spur Mt.	Puppy cr.	18 NE	2.00
" "	"	"	97	" "	" "	"	1.25
" "	"	"	9½	" "	" "	"	1.00
" "	"	"	243	" "	" "	"	3.00
Josiah Wright	Patrick	Fee	101	Spur Mt.	N Mayo	16 E	4.00

Appendix: Patrick County, Virginia, 1859 Land Tax List:

District of G, Sondefur:

Name of Owner [cont'd from prior page]	Sum added to the land on account of buildings	Total value of the land and buildings	Amount of tax on the whole tract, at the legal rate	Amount of tax for county purposes	Explanation of alterations during the preceding year, especially from whom transferred, and when and how owner derived the land	Identification
Robt Wright Decd	30.00	300.00	.80			1847 Robert Wright of Patrick County, son of 1811 William Wright of Pittsylvania County and grandson of 1755 John Wright of Lunenburg County
H. D. Wright	15.00 " "	234.00 86.00 165.00	.90 .34 .66		Transferred Wm Shelton	1887 Hiram D. Wright of Patrick County, son of 1847 Robert Wright of Patrick County, grandson of 1811 William Wright of Pittsylvania County, and great grandson of 1755 John Wright of Lunenburg County
Jubal Wright " " " "	80.00 80.00 85.00	500.00 325.00 341.00	2.00 1.30 1.36			1868 Jubal Wright of Patrick County, son of John N. Wright, grandson of 1809 Robert Wright of Patrick County, and great grandson of ____ Wright and Mary (____) Wright
Reuben Wright " " " " " "	50.00 " " 122.00	200.00 120.00 10.00 729.00	.80 .48 .04 2.52			1872 Reuben Wright of Patrick County, son of 1809 Robert Wright of Patrick County and grandson of ____ Wright and Mary (____) Wright
Josiah Wright	150.00	404.00	1.62			1862 Josiah Wright of Patrick County, son of John N. Wright, grandson of 1809 Robert Wright of Patrick County, and great grandson of ____ Wright and Mary (____) Wright

1860 LAND TAX LIST

PATRICK COUNTY, VIRGINIA

Appendix: Patrick County, Virginia, 1860 Land Tax List:

District of G. Sondefur:

Name of Owner.	Residence.	Estate, whether held in fee simple, for life, &c.	No. of Acres.	Name of Tract	Description of the land, as to water courses, mountains and contiguous tracts.	Distance and bearing from the courthouse.	Value of land per acre, including buildings
Robt Wright Decd	Patrick	Fee	50	No Name	Sycamore	7 NE	2.00
H. D. Wright	Patrick	Fee	112	No Name	Sycamore	7 NE	2.00
"	"	"	43	" "	"	" "	2.00
"	"	"	55	" "	"	" "	3.00
Jubal Wright	Patrick	Fee	100	Spur Mt.	Smiths Riv	22 NE	5.00
" "	"	"	130	" "	" "	20 "	2.50
" "	"	"	106	" "	Puppy cr.	18 "	3.22
Reuben Wright	Patrick	Fee	100	Spur Mt.	Puppy cr.	18 NE	3.22
" "	"	"	97	" "	" "	"	1.25
" "	"	"	9½	" "	" "	"	1.00
" "	"	"	243	" "	" "	"	3.00
Josiah Wright	Patrick	Fee	101	Spur Mt.	N Mayo	16 E	4.00

Appendix: Patrick County, Virginia, 1860 Land Tax List:

District of G, Sondefur:

Name of Owner [cont'd from prior page]	Sum added to the land on account of buildings	Total value of the land and buildings	Amount of tax on the whole tract, at the legal rate	Amount of tax for county purposes	Explanation of alterations during the preceding year, especially from whom transferred, and when and how owner derived the land	Identification
Robt Wright Decd	30.00	300.00	.80			1847 Robert Wright of Patrick County, son of 1811 William Wright of Pittsylvania County and grandson of 1755 John Wright of Lunenburg County
H. D. Wright	15.00 " "	222.00 86.00 165.00	.90 .34 .66			1887 Hiram D. Wright of Patrick County, son of 1847 Robert Wright of Patrick County, grandson of 1811 William Wright of Pittsylvania County, and great grandson of 1755 John Wright of Lunenburg County
Jubal Wright " " " "	80.00 80.00 85.00	500.00 325.00 341.00	2.00 1.30 1.36		Transferd from Jas. D. Martin	1868 Jubal Wright of Patrick County, son of John N. Wright, grandson of 1809 Robert Wright of Patrick County, and great grandson of ____ Wright and Mary (____) Wright
Reuben Wright " " " " " "	50.00 " " 122.00	200.00 131.00 10.00 729.00	.80 .48 .04 2.52			1872 Reuben Wright of Patrick County, son of 1809 Robert Wright of Patrick County and grandson of ____ Wright and Mary (____) Wright
Josiah Wright	150.00	404.00	1.62		A. J. & Wood _____	1862 Josiah Wright of Patrick County, son of John N. Wright, grandson of 1809 Robert Wright of Patrick County, and great grandson of ____ Wright and Mary (____) Wright

WRIGHT FAMILY RECORDS

DEATH RECORDS

1854 TO 1896

PATRICK COUNTY, VIRGINIA

Revised as of January 12, 2025

This document is an appendix to a larger work titled Sorting Some Of The Wrights Of Southern Virginia. The work is divided into parts for each family of Wrights that has been researched. Each part is divided into two sections; the first section is text discussing the family and the evidence supporting the relationships and the second section is a descendants chart summarizing the relationships and information known about each individual.

The appendices to the work (of which this document is one) present source records for persons named Wright by county and by type of record with the identification of the person named and their Wright ancestors to the extent known.

The source for the records listed in this appendix is the following:

1)   Patrick County, Virginia, Death Records, available from The Library of Virginia, 800 East Broad Street, Richmond, Virginia 23219.

2)   Patrick County, Virginia, Death Records 1868, 1869, & 1871-1896, by Barbara C. Baughan and Betty A. Pilson, Willow Bend Books, Westminster, Maryland 1999.

The identification of a person or their ancestor by year and county indicates their year of death and county of residence at death. For example, "1763 Thomas Wright of Bedford County" indicates that this was the Thomas Wright who died in 1763 in Bedford County. If no state is listed after the county, the state is Virginia; counties in states other than Virginia will have a state listed after the county, as in "1876 William S. Wright of Highland County, Ohio".

A parenthetical after the name indicates an identification of the person when a place of death is not yet known, as in "John Wright (Goochland County Carpenter)". A county in parentheses after the name indicates the county with which that person was most identified when no evidence of the place of death has yet been found, as in "Grief Wright (Bedford County)".

All or portions of the text and descendants charts for each Wright family identified are available from the author:

Robert N. Grant
15 Campo Bello Court   (H) 650-854-0895
Menlo Park, California 94025   RNG@grantandgordon.com

This is a work in progress and I would be most interested in receiving additional information about any of the persons identified in these records in order to correct any errors or expand on the information given.

Book/Page	Date	Decedent	Information	Identification
	1857/02/00	Martha J. Wright	Race: White Sex: Female Place: Patrick Cause: Typhoid Fever Age: 11 years Parents: Jubel & Emily Wright Birthplace: Smith's River Informant: Emily Wright Relationship: Mother	Martha J. Wright, daughter of 1868 Jubal Wright of Patrick County, granddaughter of John N. Wright, great granddaughter of 1809 Robert Wright of Patrick County, and great great granddaughter of _____ Wright and Mary (_____) Wright
	1857/09/00	Enorea Wright	Race: White Sex: Female Place: Patrick Cause: Typhoid Fever Age: 2 years 8 months Parents: Jubel & Emily Wright Birthplace: Smith's River Informant: Emily Wright Relationship: Mother	Enorea Wright, daughter of 1868 Jubal Wright of Patrick County, granddaughter of John N. Wright, great granddaughter of 1809 Robert Wright of Patrick County, and great great granddaughter of _____ Wright and Mary (_____) Wright
	1859/07/06	Emily W. Wright	Race: White Sex: Female Place: Patrick Co Cause: unknown Age: 36 yrs 12 days Parents: Jas & _____ Martin Birthplace: Patrick Occupation: Farmer Consort of: Consort Informant: Jubal Wright Relationship: Husband	Emily W. (Martin) Wright, wife of 1868 Jubal Wright of Patrick County, a son of John N. Wright, grandson of 1809 Robert Wright of Patrick County, and great grandson of _____ Wright and Mary (_____) Wright

Appendix: Patrick County, Virginia, Death Records

Book/Page	Date	Decedent	Information	Identification
	1860/04/08	Turner Wright	Race: White Sex: Male Place: Patrick Cause: Unknown Age: 37 Parents: John & Nancy Wright Birthplace: Patrick Occupation: Farmer Consort of: Consort Informant: Jno. __ Wright Relationship: Father	1860 Turner Wright of Patrick County, son of John N. Wright, grandson of 1809 Robert Wright of Patrick County, and great grandson of ____ Wright and Mary (____) Wright
	1860/10/24	Reuben D Wright	Race: White Sex: Male Place: Patrick Cause: Unknown Age:13 years, 1 month 24 days Parents: Wright Reuben & Delila Birthplace: Patrick Occupation: Farmer Consort of: Unmarried Informant: Reuben Wright Relationship: Father	1860 Reuben D. Wright of Patrick County, son of 1872 Reuben Wright of Patrick County, grandson of 1809 Robert Wright of Patrick County, and great grandson of ____ Wright and Mary (____) Wright
	1862/11/18	Minnesota Wright	Race: White Sex: Female Place: Patrick Co Va Cause: Dyptheria Age: 3 yrs 29 days Parents: Wright C C & Betty Birthplace: Patrick County Va Consort of: Unmarried Informant: Wright H D Relationship: God Father	Mentoria or Minnesota Wright, daughter of 1879 Columbus J. Wright of Patrick County, granddaughter of 1887 Hiram D. Wright of Patrick County, great granddaughter of 1847 Robert Wright of Patrick County, great great granddaughter of 1811 William Wright of Patrick County, and great great great granddaughter of 1755 John Wright of Lunenburg County

Book/Page	Date	Decedent	Information	Identification
	1862/10/24	____ Wright	Race: White Sex: Male Place: Patrick Co Va Cause: Unknown Age: 1 month Parents: Wright C C & Betty Birthplace: Patrick County Va Consort of: Unmarried Informant: Wright H D Relationship: God Father	_____ Wright, son of 1879 Columbus J. Wright of Patrick County, grandson of 1887 Hiram D. Wright of Patrick County, great grandson of 1847 Robert Wright of Patrick County, great great grandson of 1811 William Wright of Patrick County, and great great great grandson of.1755 John Wright of Lunenburg County
	1862/09/10	Josiah Wright	Race:White Sex: Male Place: Patrick Co Va Cause: Meningitis Age: 39 yrs 5 months 19 days Parents: John N & Mary Wright Birthplace: Patrick County Va Occupation:Unmarried Informant: Martin Wright Relationship: Brother	1862 Josiah Wright of Patrick County, son of John N. Wright, grandson of 1809 Robert Wright of Patrick County, and great grandson of ____ Wright and Mary (____) Wright
	1865/05/10	Nancy Wright	Race: White Sex: Female Place: Patrick Co Va Cause: Erysepelas(?) Age: 68 Parents: John & Mary Slaughter Birthplace: Franklin Co Va Consort of: J. N. Wright Informant: Martin Wright Relationship: Son	Nancy (Slaughter) Wright, wife of John N. Wright, a son of 1809 Robert Wright of Patrick County and grandson of ____ Wright and Mary (____) Wright

Book/Page	Date	Decedent	Information	Identification
	1865/04/17	Nancy E. Wright	Race: White Sex: Female Place: Patrick Co Va Cause: In Labor Age: 18 Parents: James & Ruth Martin Birthplace: Patrick Co Va Consort of: Wright M C Informant: M C Wright Relationship: Husband	Nancy L. (Martin) Wright, wife of 1914 Marshall C. Wright of Patrick County, a son of 1872 Reuben Wright of Patrick County, grandson of 1809 Robert Wright of Patrick County, and great grandson of _____ Wright and Mary (_____) Wright
	1866/07/05	Mary Wright	Race: White Sex: Female Place: Patrick Co Va Cause: Chronic Diarrhea Age: 64 Parents: B & N. Hughs Birthplace: Patrick Co Va Occupation: Housekeeper Consort of: H. D. Wright Informant: H. D. Wright Relationship: Husband	Mary (Hughes) Wright, wife of 1887 Hiram D. Wright of Patrick County, a son of 1847 Robert Wright of Patrick County, grandson of 1811 William Wright of Pittsylvania County, and great grandson of 1755 John Wright of Lunenburg County
	1866/07/15	Edward G Wright	Race: White Sex: Male Place: Patrick Co Va Cause: Flux Age: 2 Parents: R G & Eliza J. Wright Birthplace: Patrick Co Va Occupation: Farmer Consort of: Unmarried Informant: R G Wright Relationship: Father	

Appendix: Patrick County, Virginia, Death Records

Book/Page	Date	Decedent	Information	Identification
	1870/05/00	Martha Wright	Race: White Sex: Female Place: Patrick County Cause: Scarlet Fever Age: 6 Parent Josiah & Sally Wrights: Birthplace: Patrick Informant: Sarah Wright	Martha Wright, daughter of 1862 Josiah Wright of Patrick County, granddaughter of John N. Wright, great granddaughter of 1809 Robert Wright of Patrick County, and great great granddaughter of _____ Wright and Mary (____) Wright
	1872/11/10	Reuben Wright	Race: White Sex: Male Place: Patrick Co Cause: head dropsy Age: 62 yrs 1 month Parents: Galt(?) & Sarah Wright Birthplace: King Wm Co Occupation: Farmer Consort of: Informant: Deliah Relationship: Wife	1872 Reuben Wright of Patrick County, son of 1809 Robert Wright of Patrick County and grandson of _____ Wright and Mary (____) Wright
	1879/06/01	C. J. Wright	Race: White Sex: Male Place: Patrick Co Cause: abcess of Lungs Age: 45 Parents: H. D. & Mary Wright Birthplace: Patrick Co Occupation: Farmer Consort of: Informant: Betty Wright Relationship:	1879 Columbus J. Wright of Patrick County, son of 1887 Hiram D. Wright of Patrick County, grandson of 1847 Robert Wright of Patrick County, great grandson of 1811 William Wright of Pittsylvania County, and great great grandson of 1755 John Wright of Lunenburg County

Appendix: Patrick County, Virginia, Death Records

Book/Page	Date	Decedent	Information	Identification
	1880/05/15	Elizabeth Wright	Race: White Sex: Female Place: Patrick Cause: Dropsy Age: 25 Parents: Unknown Birthplace: Unknown Occupation: Housekeeper Consort of: Consort Informant: Nathan B Terry Relationship: Supt of Poor	
	1885/10/03	Nancy Jane Wright	Race: White Sex: Female Place: Patrick Cause: Suicide by Hanging Age: 39 Parents Fleming & Polley Via Birthplace: Patrick Occupation: Housekeeper Consort of: J. N. Wright Informant: J. N. Wright Relationship: Husband	Nancy Jane (Via) Wright, wife of 1920 Jefferson Nash Wright of Patrick Count, a son of 1872 Reuben Wright of Patrick County, grandson of 1809 Robert Wright of Patrick County, and great grandson of _____ Wright and Mary (_____) Wright
	1887/08/13	H. D. Wright	Race: White Sex: Male Cause: Chronic Diarrhea Place: Patrick Cause: Heart(?) dropsy Age: 83 Parents: Robert & Mary Wright Birthplace: Pittsylvania Occupation: Farmer Consort of: Mary Wright Informant: M __ Wright Relationship: Wife	1887 Hiram D. Wright of Patrick County, son of 1847 Robert Wright of Patrick County, grandson of 1811 William Wright of Pittsylvania County, and great grandson of 1755 John Wright of Lunenburg County

Book/Page	Date	Decedent	Information	Identification
	1889/04/06	Henry S Wright	Race: White Sex: Male Place: Patrick Co Va Cause: Consumption Age: 62 Parents Wm & Fitney Wright Birthplace: Patrick Co Occupation: Farmer Consort of: Consort of Informant: Lucy Relationship: Head of Family	1889 Henry Sanders Wright of Patrick County, son of 1861 William Green Wright of Patrick County, grandson of 1840 Richard P. Wright of Pittsylvania County, great grandson of 1811 William Wright of Pittsylvania County, and great great grandson of 1755 John Wright of Lunenburg County
	1889/04/17	Peter J Wright	Race: White Sex: Male Place: Marion Asilum Cause: Fitts & Insanty Age: 16 Parents: S Green & Susan Wright Birthplace: Patrick County Occupation: Consort of: Informant: S G Wright Relationship: Father	1889 Peter J. Wright of Patrick County, son of 1904 Squire Green Wright of Patrick County, grandson of 1872 Reuben Wright of Patrick County, great grandson of 1809 Robert Wright of Patrick County, and great great grandson of _____ Wright and Mary (____) Wright
	1889/08/24	James P Wright	Race: White Sex: Male Place: Patrick County Cause: Lock of Bowels Age: 55 yrs 8 mos Parents: Ruben & Mary F Wright Birthplace: Patrick County Occupation: Farmer Consort of: Mary Wright Informant: Mary Wright Relationship: Wife	1889 James Patterson Wright of Patrick County, son of 1872 Reuben Wright of Patrick County, grandson of 1809 Robert Wright of Patrick County and great grandson of _____ Wright and Mary (____) Wright

Appendix: Patrick County, Virginia, Death Records

Book/Page	Date	Decedent	Information	Identification
	1891/01/02	America Wright	Race: White Sex: Female Place: near Charity Va Cause:Consumption Age: 39 Parents: Geo & Susannah Thomas Birthplace: Franklin Co Occupation: Housekeeper Consort of: Wm F Wright Informant: Wm F Wright Relationship: Head of Family	America (Thomas) Wright, wife of 1920/21 William Floyd Wright (Patrick County), a son of 1872 Reuben Wright of Patrick County, grandson of 1809 Robert Wright of Patrick County, and great grandson of _____ Wright and Mary (_____) Wright
	1892/05/18	Victoria S Wright	Race: White Sex: Female Place: Patrick Co Cause: Whooping Cough Age: 17 Parents: Wm F & America Wright Birthplace: Patrick Co Occupation: Housekeeper Consort of: Unmarried Informant: Wm F. Wright Relationship: Head of family	Louisa Victoria Wright, daughter of 1920/21 William Floyd Wright (Patrick County), granddaughter of 1872 Reuben Wright of Patrick County, great granddaughter of 1809 Robert Wriight of Patrick County, and great great granddaughter of _____ Wright and Mary (_____) Wright
	1892/06/03	Peyton B. Wright	Race: White Sex: Male Place: Patrick Co Cause: Membranous Croup Age: 5 yrs 18 days Parents: Jeff N & Annie L Wright Birthplace: Patrick Co Informant: J. N. Wright Relationship: Head of family	1892 Peyton Ross or B. Wright of Patrick County, son of 1920 Jefferson Nash Wright of Patrick County, grandson of 1872 Reuben Wright of Patrick County, great grandson of 1809 Robert Wright of Patrick County, and great great grandson of _____ Wright and Mary (_____) Wright

Book/Page	Date	Decedent	Information	Identification
	1895/03/15	Mary D. Wright	Race: White Sex: Female Place: Patrick County Cause: Hooping Cough Age: 8 yrs 13 days Parents: J M & Ellen F Wright Birthplace: Patrick County Occupation: none Consort of: none Informant: Ellen Wright Relationship: Mother of (dec)	Mary D. Wright, daughter of Joshua M. Wright, granddaughter of 1900 Martin Wright of Patrick County, great granddaughter of John N. Wright, great great granddaughter of 1809 Robert Wright of Patrick County, and great great great granddaughter of _____ Wright and Mary (_____) Wright
	1895/05/13	Martha E. Wright	Race: White Sex: Female Place: Patrick County Cause: Consumption Age: 6 years 7 days Parents: J M & Ellen F Wright Birthplace: Patrick County Occupation: none Consort of: none Informant: Ellen Wright Relationship: Mother of (dec)	Martha E. Wright, daughter of Joshua M. Wright, granddaughter of 1900 Martin Wright of Patrick County, great granddaughter of John N. Wright, great great granddaughter of 1809 Robert Wright of Patrick County, and great great great granddaughter of _____ Wright and Mary (_____) Wright

WRIGHT FAMILY RECORDS

PROBATE RECORDS

1790 TO 1870

PATRICK COUNTY, VIRGINIA

Revised as of January 12, 2025

This document is an appendix to a larger work titled <u>Sorting Some Of The Wrights Of Southern Virginia</u>. The work is divided into parts for each family of Wrights that has been researched. Each part is divided into two sections; the first section is text discussing the family and the evidence supporting the relationships and the second section is a descendants chart summarizing the relationships and information known about each individual.

The appendices to the work (of which this document is one) present source records for persons named Wright by county and by type of record with the identification of the person named and their Wright ancestors to the extent known.

The source for the records listed in this appendix is the following:

1) Patrick County, Virginia, Probate Records, available from the Clerk of the Circuit Court, P.O. Box 148, Stuart, Virginia 24171-0148.

The identification of a person or their ancestor by year and county indicates their year of death and county of residence at death. For example, "1763 Thomas Wright of Bedford County" indicates that this was the Thomas Wright who died in 1763 in Bedford County. If no state is listed after the county, the state is Virginia; counties in states other than Virginia will have a state listed after the county, as in "1876 William S. Wright of Highland County, Ohio".

A parenthetical after the name indicates an identification of the person when a place of death is not yet known, as in "John Wright (Goochland County Carpenter)". A county in parentheses after the name indicates the county with which that person was most identified when no evidence of the place of death has yet been found, as in "Grief Wright (Bedford County)".

All or portions of the text and descendants charts for each Wright family identified are available from the author:

Robert N. Grant
15 Campo Bello Court   (H) 650-854-0895
Menlo Park, California 94025   RNG@grantandgordon.com

This is a work in progress and I would be most interested in receiving additional information about any of the persons identified in these records in order to correct any errors or expand on the information given.

Appendix: Patrick County, Virginia, Probate Records

Book/Page	Date	Decedent	Document	Identification
001 107	07/00/1809	Robert Wright or Write	Will	1809 Robert Wright of Patrick County, son of ____ Wright and Mary (____) Wright
001 251	08/01/1809	Robert Wright or Write	Invt. & Appr.	1809 Robert Wright of Patrick County, son of ____ Wright and Mary (____) Wright
004 162	04/29/1814	Robert Wright	Account Current	1809 Robert Wright of Patrick County, son of ____ Wright and Mary (____) Wright
003 402	1847	Robert Wright	Sale Bill	1847 Robert Wright of Patrick County, son of 1811 William Wright of Pittsylvania County and grandson of 1755 John Wright of Lunenburg County
003 466	1847	Robert Wright	Invt. & Appr.	1847 Robert Wright of Patrick County, son of 1811 William Wright of Pittsylvania County and grandson of 1755 John Wright of Lunenburg County
003 505	1847	Robert Wright	Will	1847 Robert Wright of Patrick County, son of 1811 William Wright of Pittsylvania County and grandson of 1755 John Wright of Lunenburg County
004 024	1849	Robert Wright	Account Current	1847 Robert Wright of Patrick County, son of 1811 William Wright of Pittsylvania County and grandson of 1755 John Wright of Lunenburg County
004 130	1850	Sarah Wright	Invt. & Appr.	Sarah (____) Wright, wife of 1809 Robert Wright of Patrick County, a son of ____ Wright and Mary (____) Wright
004 145	1845	Sarah Wright	Will	Sarah (____) Wright, wife of 1809 Robert Wright of Patrick County, a son of ____ Wright and Mary (____) Wright
004 174	1852	Sarah Wright	Sale Bill	Sarah (____) Wright, wife of 1809 Robert Wright of Patrick County, a son of ____ Wright and Mary (____) Wright

Appendix: Patrick County, Virginia, Probate Records

Book/Page		Date	Decedent	Document	Identification
006	131	1862	William Wright	Invt. & Appr.	1861 William Wright of Patrick County, son of 1840 Richard P. Wright of Pittsylvania County, grandson of 1811 William Wright of Pittsylvania County, and great grandson of 1755 John Wright of Lunenburg County
006	203	1863	Josiah Wright	Invt. & Appr.	1862 Josiah Wright of Patrick County, son of John N. Wright, grandson of 1809 Robert Wright of Patrick County, and great grandson of _____ Wright and Mary (_____) Wright
006	265	1863	Robert Wright	Sale Bill	1847 Robert Wright of Patrick County, son of 1811 William Wright of Pittsylvania County and grandson of 1755 John Wright of Lunenburg County
006	573	1868	Jubal Wright	Invt. & Appr.	1868 Jubal Wright of Patrick County, son of John N. Wright, grandson of 1809 Robert Wright of Patrick County, and great grandson of _____ Wright and Mary (_____) Wright
007	140	1870	Robert Wright	Account Current	1847 Robert Wright of Patrick County, son of 1811 William Wright of Pittsylvania County and grandson of 1755 John Wright of Lunenburg County